The Complete Olympic Games Quiz Book

Also by Martin Greensill

Summer Olympics Quiz Book
The Ultimate Sports Quiz Book

THE COMPLETE OLYMPIC GAMES QUIZ BOOK

Martin Greensill

The Complete Olympic Games Quiz Book

ISBN 978-1-291-06015-7

Printed in the United Kingdom

First edition and printing, September 2012

Cover photographs from Wikimedia Commons

DEDICATION

This book is dedicated to the memory of British athlete Lillian Board (1948–1970), who won a silver medal at the 1968 Summer Olympics in Mexico City but was denied the chance to compete at further Games, and indeed to continue her outstanding career, by her tragically premature death only two years later.

To live in the hearts of those we love is never to die.
(Thomas Campbell)

CONTENTS

PREFACE

This title is based on my earlier *Summer Olympics Quiz Book* but is a much larger, revised and updated work. While presenting hundreds of facts about the Olympic Games, I hope to have done so in a way that is both informative and entertaining. In particular, I hope to have revived memories of the drama and excitement that lit up London 2012 and previous Olympics and have helped make the event what is today: the greatest spectacle in world sport and the pinnacle of many a sporting career.

Martin Greensill
September 2012

PART A –

SUMMER OLYMPICS QUESTIONS

1. Summer Olympic History

Part 1 – Overview
1. In which Greek city were the first Ancient Olympic Games held in 776 BC?
2. Which small town in Shropshire is regarded as the birthplace of the modern Olympics, having helped revive the Olympic ideal by staging an 'Olympian Games' from 1850 onwards?
3. Founder of the International Olympic Committee (IOC), which Frenchman is considered the 'father' of the modern Olympic Games?
4. Which city hosted the first modern Olympics in 1896?
5. Name the first city in the southern hemisphere to stage a Summer Olympics.
6. The Oscar-winning film *Chariots of Fire* (1981) portrays athletics events at what year's Summer Games?
7. Name the first Asian city to stage a Summer Olympics.
8. In which two years prior to 2012 had London hosted a Summer Olympic Games?
9. Five nations have competed at every Summer Olympics: Australia, France, Greece, Great Britain, and which other?
10. Only five sports have been contested at every Summer Games: athletics, cycling, gymnastics, swimming, and what other?

Answers on page 195

Part 2 – Recent history (1980–2012)

1. Which major international event prompted the United States to lead a boycott of the 1980 Summer Olympics?
2. Name the athletics star who won four gold medals at the 1984 Games in Los Angeles.
3. An American 'Dream Team' competed successfully in which sport at Barcelona 1992?
4. What spectator-friendly sport, with two players per side, was added to the programme for the 1996 Atlanta Olympics?
5. At the Sydney Games of 2000, which Australian athlete won the women's 400m title in front of a record Olympic crowd?
6. In which two athletics events did Britain's Kelly Holmes take gold at the 2004 Athens Olympics?
7. How many gold medals did American swimmer Michael Phelps win at the 2008 Beijing Games?
8. What three-word phrase was the official motto of the 2012 London Games?
9. Which city will host the 2016 Summer Olympics?
10. In May 2012, the IOC announced a shortlist of which three cities as candidates to host the 2020 Summer Games?

Answers on page 195

The Modern Games

Athens 1896

1. Name the Greek monarch who officially opened these Games.
2. Which two new sporting events (both part of the athletics programme) were introduced in Athens?
3. Winners of events here were in fact awarded a silver medal, rather than a gold one, while runners-up were given a medal made from what metal?
4. The first modern Olympic champion was James Connolly (USA), who won which field event in athletics in 1896?
5. The most successful competitor was Germany's Carl Schumann, who gained three titles in gymnastics and one in which other sport?
6. Leonidas Pyrgos became Greece's first Olympic champion of the modern era with victory in what sport?
7. Born in Ireland, which at the time was part of the United Kingdom, John Boland claimed two titles for Great Britain when competing in which sport?
8. Greece's Spyridon Louis delighted the home crowd by winning which athletics event?
9. Following the cancellation of the planned rowing and sailing events, what was the only sport that took place in the Bay of Zea, near the Athens port of Piraeus?
10. Which country topped the medal table in Athens?

Answers on page 196

Paris 1900

1. These Olympics were held as part of which major international event of 1900?
2. The first female Olympian, Swiss noblewoman Hélène, Countess de Pourtalès, also became the first female Olympic medallist when she won team gold and silver medals in what sport?
3. The athletics events at these Games took place on which surface for the only time in Olympic history?
4. In a feat still unsurpassed in Olympic athletics, which US competitor claimed four individual titles at these Games?
5. Name the American standing jumps expert who began his outstanding Olympic career by winning three gold medals on the same day.
6. The winner of the marathon, Michel Théato, was long thought to have been French but was in fact a citizen of what neighbouring country?
7. Which Normandy port staged some of the sailing events?
8. The croquet and tug of war events took place in which Paris park?
9. George Orton's gold and bronze in athletics were the first ever medals for what nation?
10. The British team Moseley Wanderers made a day-trip to Paris and returned home with a silver medal from which sport?

Answers on page 196

St Louis 1904

1. The venue for these Olympics was changed by the IOC after it had originally chosen which other American city as the host?
2. Which US president requested this change so that these Games could be held in conjunction with the 1904 World's Fair?
3. Anton Heida (USA) was the most successful competitor in St Louis, winning five gold medals in what sport?
4. A swimming club from which US city won most swimming titles, outperforming even Russia and Hungary?
5. In athletics, who won the 1500 metres in world record time and claimed two other titles on the track?
6. The youngest champion in St Louis, 17-year-old American Robert Hunter, was successful in which sport?
7. Which country claimed the football title in 1904 but failed to add another Olympic medal in this sport for over a century?
8. The most successful non-American competitor was Germany's Emil Rausch, the winner of three events in what sport?
9. Frederick Lorz (USA) crossed the finishing line first in the marathon but was disqualified after it was discovered he had covered the last 11 miles of the course by which underhand method?
10. What Caribbean nation finished third in the medal table, still its highest placing in Olympic history?

Answers on page 197

Athens 1906 (Intercalated Games)

1. The opening ceremony of these Games saw which innovation that became a feature at every subsequent Olympics?
2. As in 1896, which Athens stadium was the centrepiece of these Games?
3. What nation sent its first official team, thereby ending the practice of entries from individuals, colleges and clubs?
4. Switzerland's Louis Richardet was the most successful competitor in Athens, winning three gold and three silver medals in what sport?
5. Although still part of the Russian Empire, which European nation marked its Olympic debut by taking a discus title in athletics?
6. Which American runner claimed both the 400 and 800m titles, a feat unmatched in Olympic athletics until 1976?
7. Great Britain's Henry Hawtrey won which track title in athletics that is no longer an Olympic event and was raced over an imperial distance rather than a metric one?
8. What European country collected six medals in tennis, including gold in the women's singles?
9. Name the Swedish athlete who won gold in the javelin and bronze medals in the shot put and tug of war.
10. Which Irish-born New York City policeman showed his all-round prowess by triumphing in the shot put and discus and finishing runner-up in three other events?

Answers on page 197

London 1908

1. Who officially opened these Olympics?
2. Specially built for the purpose, what was the main stadium used for these Games?
3. Which team sport made its first appearance at these Olympics?
4. In what sport did Great Britain win all but one of the 15 medals on offer?
5. Name the Italian runner who crossed the finishing line first in the marathon but was disqualified for receiving assistance after collapsing five times in the stadium and being helped to complete the race.
6. Which famous writer witnessed the dramatic conclusion of the marathon when reporting for a newspaper?
7. In what sport did Denmark beat France by a resounding 17–1 scoreline?
8. Nikolai Panin became Russia's first ever Olympic champion when taking gold in what *winter* sport?
9. Which American swimmer took his tally of Olympic medals to eight with victory in the 100 metres freestyle?
10. What European nation placed third in the medal table behind Great Britain and the United States?

Answers on page 198

Stockholm 1912

1. In 1912, which nation became both the first Arab and first African nation to compete at the Olympics?
2. What European country made its Olympic bow but, in a tragic twist of fate, saw one of its competitors die after he collapsed while competing in the marathon?
3. Sweden, as the host country, refused to allow which sport at these Games?
4. Women's events were introduced here in which two aquatic sports?
5. Name the American star who was hailed as 'the greatest athlete in the world' by King Gustav V of Sweden after claiming both the pentathlon and decathlon titles.
6. What athletics event was won in world record time by Ted Meredith of the United States?
7. Britain's only individual champion in athletics in Stockholm, Arnold Jackson raced to a surprise victory in which track event?
8. Three French brothers, the Thubés, took gold in what sport?
9. In an all-European affair, who did Great Britain beat 4–2 in the final of the football tournament?
10. The longest event in Olympic history, a 320km cycling road race, was won by Okey Lewis, a competitor for which country?

Answers on page 198

Antwerp 1920

1. What was introduced at these Olympics and has been taken by athletes at every Games since then?
2. Name either of the two *winter* sports in which medals were awarded at the 1920 Summer Olympics.
3. The most successful competitor here was Willis Lee (USA), the winner of seven medals, including five gold, in what sport?
4. Which Briton claimed the 800 and 1500 metres titles in athletics, completing the last Olympic double in these events for 44 years?
5. Name the American sprinter who won the 100m in athletics, delighting fans with a spectacular jump finish.
6. The youngest champion in Antwerp was a 14-year-old American, Aileen Riggin, who was successful in what aquatic sport?
7. Sport shooter Guilherme Paraense became the first ever Olympic champion from which South American nation?
8. Uniquely in Olympic history, an event in what sport was held in two different countries?
9. Nicknamed 'La Divine' (The Divine One), which flamboyant Frenchwoman won two golds in tennis at these Games?
10. Which European country marked its Olympic debut as an independent nation by taking 15 golds and finishing fourth in the medal table?

Answers on page 199

Paris 1924

1. Which Olympic motto was introduced at these Games by the IOC?
2. What was the name of the Olympic Stadium where the opening ceremony and events in several sports were held?
3. The 1981 film *Chariots of Fire* tells the story of which two British Olympic champions from these Games?
4. Frenchman Roger Ducret collected five medals, including three gold, in which sport?
5. Harold Osborn (USA) was hailed as the 'world's greatest athlete' after winning the decathlon and what other athletics title?
6. Which Finnish runner won four golds in 1924 but was still outshone by a famous team-mate who won five?
7. Who won three golds in swimming and a bronze in water polo and later enjoyed a successful career as a Hollywood actor?
8. Argentina gained its first ever Olympic gold medal when successful in which outdoor team sport?
9. Silver medallist Pete Desjardins (USA) became the first Olympic competitor to achieve a perfect 10 score in what sport?
10. The oldest medallist in Paris, which American tennis player took gold at the age of 37 and later had a tennis trophy named after her?

Answers on page 199

Amsterdam 1928

1. These Games saw the first female participation at the Olympics in athletics and which other sport?
2. Halina Konopacka of Poland became the first female Olympic champion in athletics when she won what field event in 1928?
3. Japan's Mikio Oda became the first Asian individual Olympic champion when taking gold in which athletics field event?
4. Sprinter Percy Williams completed a 100-200m double in athletics competing for what nation?
5. Pat O'Callaghan made history as the first Olympic champion representing Ireland when he took gold in which field event in athletics?
6. What country won the men's hockey tournament without conceding a goal?
7. Which South American nation retained its football title with a win over its bitterest rivals in a replayed final?
8. The oldest champion in Amsterdam, France's Virginie Hériot took gold in which sport aged 38?
9. The youngest female medallist in Olympic history, Italy's Luigina Giavotti earned a silver medal in what sport at the tender age of 11?
10. Which nation marked its return to the Olympic fold by placing second in the medal table behind the USA?

Answers on page 200

Los Angeles 1932

1. These Games were officially opened by Charles Curtis, the holder of which high-ranking political office?
2. The male competitors here were housed in a specially built Olympic 'village', but what type of accommodation was provided for their female colleagues?
3. Which South American nation made its Olympic debut in Los Angeles?
4. Name the California harbour that staged the sailing events.
5. What innovation for track races in athletics was introduced at these Games?
6. Great Britain's women's athletics team marked their Olympic debut with a bronze medal in which track event?
7. What nation claimed all 12 titles on offer in the diving competition?
8. Swedish policeman Ivar Johansson won two golds in which sport?
9. In what sport did Hungary beat Japan by an Olympic record score of 18–0?
10. A Japanese team in which sport broke the world record by a remarkable 37.8 seconds when taking gold?

Answers on page 200

Berlin 1936

1. Which European country boycotted these Games for political reasons and organized an alternative 'People's Olympiad'?
2. Despite holding the national record in the high jump, Gretel Bergmann was excluded from Germany's Olympic team for what reason?
3. Games organiser Carl Diem was responsible for what innovation that has featured at all Olympics since 1936?
4. What was the capacity of the Olympic Stadium specially built for these Games?
5. Glenn Morris (USA), who later found movie fame as Tarzan, claimed which athletics title in Berlin?
6. Which German athlete befriended Jesse Owens during the long jump competition and, in a fine display of sportsmanship, gave the American star some advice that helped him qualify for the final?
7. What athletics event did the New Zealand runner Jack Lovelock win in world record time?
8. France's Robert Carpentier took three gold medals in which sport?
9. In what sport did of Hendrika Mastenbroek of the Netherlands win three golds and a silver?
10. In what sport did Germany's Konrad Frey and Alfred Schwarzmann both claim three titles?

Answers on page 201

London 1948

1. Which two-man European team received a rousing ovation at the opening ceremony in Wembley Stadium?
2. Described as "tall and handsome like a young Greek god", who failed to make the Great Britain athletics team for the Games but was controversially chosen to light the Olympic Cauldron in the stadium?
3. Name the only two sports in which Great Britain won Olympic gold in 1948.
4. The leading performer was Finland's Veikko Huhtanen, who took three golds, a silver and a bronze in which sport?
5. Alice Coachman (USA) became the first black female Olympic champion when successful in what athletics event?
6. Runner-up in the 400 metre hurdles, Duncan White was the first ever Olympic medallist for which south-east Asian country?
7. What Caribbean nation marked its Olympic debut by taking three medals in athletics?
8. In which sport did Hungary's Ilona Elek retain her title from the 1936 Berlin Games?
9. What nationality was the sailor Magnus Konow, who competed at these Games a remarkable 40 years after making his Olympic debut?
10. Which future legend of the sport managed the Great Britain football team at these Olympics?

Answers on page 201

Helsinki 1952

1. What nation made its Olympic debut in 1952 after first competing under a different name 40 years earlier?
2. Paavo Nurmi and which other Finnish athletics hero jointly lit the Olympic Cauldron during the opening ceremony?
3. Which Australian sprinter set world records when winning the women's 100 and 200m titles – but ruined her chances of a third gold when she dropped the baton in the 4x100m final?
4. Also in athletics, for which small European country did Josy Barthel pull off a shock victory in the men's 1500m final?
5. The oldest medallist in Helsinki, 58-year-old Frenchman André Jousseaume won an individual bronze in what sport?
6. A Korean-American, Sammy Lee, became the first man to defend an Olympic title in which aquatic sport?
7. Which future world champion was disqualified for not "giving of his best" after failing to throw a punch in the heavyweight boxing final?
8. The first woman to win an Olympic medal in equestrian, Lis Hartel won silver in the dressage despite being paralysed below the knee. Which Scandinavian country did she represent?
9. Name the famous horse that helped Great Britain gain its only gold medal in Helsinki.
10. Which European nation won 24 medals but, for the only time when competing at a Summer Games, no golds?

Answers on page 202

Melbourne 1956

1. The Netherlands, Spain and Switzerland all withdrew from these Olympics in protest at which major international event?
2. Due to Australia's strict quarantine regulations, what European city staged the equestrian events for these Games?
3. Which member of the British royal family officially opened the Games in Melbourne?
4. Ireland gained its first Olympic title since 1932 when Ronnie Delany won which track event in athletics?
5. Which Australian athlete retained her 80m hurdles title and won gold in the sprint relay to end her Olympic career with a total of seven medals?
6. Hungary's László Papp become the first competitor in what sport to claim a title at three consecutive Olympics?
7. Although a member of a combined team, Wolfgang Behrendt became the first Olympic champion from which country after taking gold in the bantamweight division in boxing?
8. What nationality was Gunhild Larking, a beautiful high jumper who was the most photographed competitor at the Games?
9. The oldest gold medallist here, 54-year-old Henry St Cyr of Sweden, was successful in which sport?
10. The idea of an Australian teenager, what innovation first appeared at the closing ceremony and has featured ever since?

Answers on page 202

Rome 1960

1. Making full use of Rome's architectural splendour, which athletics event began at the Capitol Hill and ended near the Arch of Constantine?
2. What bay was the picturesque setting for the sailing events at these Games?
3. The top performer here was Boris Shakhlin (USSR), who took seven medals, including four golds, in which sport?
4. Name the fire insurance clerk from London who was the only Briton to win an athletics title in Rome.
5. Which Australian runner broke his own world record when taking 1500m gold in sparkling style?
6. Which American sprinter was hailed as 'the fastest woman in the world' after winning three gold medals on the track?
7. What country ended India's run of six successive hockey titles, in the process taking its first ever Olympic gold in any sport?
8. In boxing, which future sporting legend defeated Poland's Zbigniew Pietrzykowski to win light heavyweight gold?
9. Jeff Farrell of the United States won two titles in what sport after undergoing an emergency appendectomy six days before the US Olympic Trials of August 1960?
10. In sailing, the future king of which European country took gold in the Dragon class?

Answers on page 203

Tokyo 1964

1. What was the name of the Japanese emperor who officially opened these Games?
2. The Olympic torch was brought into the stadium by a runner born near which Japanese city on the day in 1945 when an atomic bomb had been dropped over it?
3. Which two sports, both popular in Japan, were introduced to the programme for Tokyo?
4. Name the New Zealander who completed the first 800-1500m double in athletics since 1920.
5. Which US sprinter won 100m gold in world record time and then took his country to victory in the 4x100m relay?
6. Great Britain celebrated its first ever Olympic champion in women's athletics when Mary Rand won what event with a world record performance?
7. Galina Prozumenschikova became the first competitor from the Soviet Union to claim an Olympic title in which sport?
8. In boxing, which future world champion won the heavyweight crown despite fighting with a damaged hand after breaking a thumb in his semi-final bout?
9. In what sport did Hungary's Imre Polyák finally win a gold medal after being runner-up in the same event at the three previous Olympics?
10. Which nation was a notable absentee from these Games and did not return to the Olympic fold until 1992?

Answers on page 203

Mexico City 1968

1. On 2 October 1968, ten days before the start of the Games, dozens of protesters were killed during a peaceful demonstration in Mexico City. By what name is this incident known?
2. How did Mexican hurdler Enriqueta Basilio make Olympic history at the opening ceremony of these Games?
3. What famous resort hosted the sailing events?
4. In athletics, who won gold in the men's high jump using a revolutionary new technique?
5. East Germany's Klaus Beer was the almost forgotten runner-up to which world record breaker at these Games?
6. Who claimed Great Britain's only gold medal in athletics when he raced to victory in world record time?
7. Soviet husband and wife Mikhail and Sinaida Voronin won a combined total of 11 medals in which sport?
8. Debbie Meyer (USA) became the first competitor to win three individual gold medals at the same Games in what sport?
9. American Janice Romary became the first woman to compete at six Olympics when she took part in which sport?
10. Which Asian country placed third in the medal table behind the United States and the Soviet Union?

Answers on page 204

Munich 1972

1. On the eve of the Games, what nation had its invitation to compete withdrawn by the IOC after intense pressure from black African countries protesting against this nation's racial policies?
2. What was the name of the terrorist group that killed eleven Israelis in the so-called 'Munich Massacre'?
3. Name either of the sports that returned to the Olympic programme after a long absence.
4. Which 15-year-old female Australian swimmer won five medals, including three golds?
5. Which Soviet sprinter became the first European athlete to complete a 100-200m double at the Olympics?
6. In what event did Mary Peters win Great Britain's only gold medal in athletics?
7. What African nation claimed the last athletics title of the Games with victory in the men's 4x400m relay?
8. Name the British equestrian who won two gold medals in Munich, taking his overall Olympic total to three golds.
9. Aleksandr Medved (USSR) claimed his third consecutive Olympic title in what indoor sport?
10. After placing third in the team race, four cyclists from which European country were disqualified for taking performance enhancing drugs?

Answers on page 204

Montreal 1976

1. An African-led boycott of these Games was precipitated by a tour of South Africa by a rugby union team from what country?
2. Name either of the ball sports in which women were allowed to compete for the first time at an Olympics?
3. Which 15-year old Romanian gymnast was the star of the Games after winning three gold medals and achieving seven perfect 10 scores?
4. Great Britain won its first gold in swimming since 1960 when David Wilkie took which title?
5. Which East European nation claimed a record sixth title in water polo?
6. Name the female Soviet runner who completed the first women's 800-1500 metres double in Olympic history.
7. Who became the first runner to achieve a 400-800m double at the same Olympics since the Interim Games of 1906?
8. Italian brothers Raimondo and Piero D'Inzeo competed at their eighth successive Olympics in what sport ?
9. Competing against men, Margaret Murdock (USA) made history as the first female Olympic medallist in which sport?
10. In what sport were three medallists disqualified after failing drug tests?

Answers on page 205

Moscow 1980

1. Name the Soviet leader who officially opened these Games.
2. Now the capital of an independent country, which Baltic port staged the sailing events in 1980?
3. In athletics, who became first Great Britain's first Olympic 100 metres champion since 1924?
4. Nicknamed 'The Shifter', which Ethiopian athlete completed a superb 5000m-10000m double at these Games?
5. Which Cuban heavyweight (who died in June 2012) became the first boxer to win the same Olympic title three times?
6. Vladimir Parfenovich (USSR) became the first competitor to win three gold medals at a single Games in which aquatic sport?
7. In swimming, which East German woman claimed three gold medals in world record times but was later revealed to have taken performance enhancing drugs?
8. Name the swimming event in which Duncan Goodhew struck gold for Britain.
9. Which East European country won the football tournament for the only time in Olympic history?
10. What was the name of the bear character that was used as the mascot for these Games?

Answers on page 205

Los Angeles 1984

1. How did Bill Suitor make a dramatic arrival at the opening ceremony of these Games?
2. The cauldron was lit by Rafer Johnson, a former Olympic champion in which sport?
3. Name either of the two sports in which events for women were introduced in 1984.
4. In gymnastics, which 16-year-old American became the first gymnast from outside Eastern Europe to win the women's all-around competition?
5. In athletics, which female US runner became the first athlete of either gender to complete a 200-400m double at the same Olympics?
6. Carlos Lopes won the men's marathon to become the first ever Olympic champion for what country?
7. Xu Haifang claimed China's first ever Olympic title when taking gold in which sport?
8. Which female British equestrian marked her Olympic debut by gaining two medals in three-day eventing?
9. Name the famous stadium in Pasadena, California, that staged the football final.
10. After refusing to join the Soviet-led boycott of the Games, which East European nation won 20 golds and placed second in the medal table behind the USA?

Answers on page 206

Seoul 1988

1. Which Japanese city did Seoul defeat in the bid election to host these Games?
2. The opening ceremony featured a mass demonstration of which Korean martial art, with hundreds of adults and children performing moves in unison?
3. What sport was reintroduced as a medal sport for the first time since 1924?
4. In athletics, which female US sprinter won three gold medals and twice broke the world record in the 200 metres?
5. Who took gold in the men's 100m after the original winner, Ben Johnson of Canada, was sensationally disqualified for failing a drug test?
6. Name the British middle distance runner who placed second in the men's 1500 metres.
7. Peter Seisenbacher of Austria and Japan's Htoshi Saito became the first repeat Olympic champions in what sport?
8. Italian brothers Carmine, Giuseppe and Agostino Abbagale all earned medals in which sport?
9. Denmark's Paul Elvstrøm and Durward Knowles of the Bahamas both competed in what sport for a joint-record eighth time at an Olympics?
10. The Soviet Union topped the medal table with 55 golds but which nation placed second?

Answers on page 206

Barcelona 1992

1. How did paraplegic sportsman Antonio Rebollo make a spectacular contribution to the opening ceremony?
2. Following the break-up of the Soviet Union, which Baltic state competed as an independent nation at the Summer Olympics for the first time since 1928?
3. The diving events and the water polo preliminaries were held in an outdoor swimming pool overlooked by which famous Barcelona landmark?
4. Hungarian teenager Krisztina Egerszegi won three individual gold medals in what sport?
5. In athletics, Kevin Young (USA) was victorious in which track event with a stunning world record that still stands today?
6. Name the winners of the inaugural Olympic baseball title.
7. Which Australian swimmer smashed the world record when claiming the men's 1500m freestyle title?
8. Who took gold in the women's singles tennis competition at the age of 16?
9. The oldest champion was Germany's Klaus Balkenhol, who was successful in which sport aged 52?
10. A judging mix-up in what aquatic sport later led to Canada's Sylvia Frechette being promoted to joint gold medallist?

Answers on page 207

Atlanta 1996

1. Which city on the Georgia coast staged the sailing events at these Games?
2. The most successful competitor in Atlanta was Amy Van Dyken (USA), who won four golds in which sport?
3. In athletics, who took the men's 200 metres in world record time and the 400 metres in Olympic record time?
4. Which Canadian sprinter won 100m gold in world record time and then anchored his team to victory in the 4x100m relay final?
5. Name the famous sporting duo who earned Great Britain its only gold medal of these Games.
6. Frenchwoman Jeannie Longo was victorious in which sport at the age of 37?
7. In tennis, who won the men's singles to complete a career 'Golden Slam', adding Olympic gold to his singles titles at the four grand slam tournaments?
8. Who partnered Tim Henman as Great Britain took silver in the men's doubles in tennis?
9. Which South American country was runner-up to Nigeria in the men's football tournament?
10. The oldest competitor in Atlanta, Faustino Puccini of Italy took part in what sport at the age of 63?

Answers on page 207

Sydney 2000

1. Which Asian country was banned by the IOC from competing at these Games on account of its rulers' restrictions on women and prohibition of sports?
2. As part of a spectacular opening ceremony, who lit the flame in the Olympic cauldron within a circle of fire?
3. Dutchman Leontien Ziljaard was one of the star performers with three individual gold medals in what sport?
4. At the age of 39, Ellina Zvereva of Belarus won which field event to become the oldest individual female champion in the history of Olympic athletics?
5. Which Ethiopian distance runner retained his 10000m title after a thrilling duel with Kenya's Paul Tergat?
6. For which European nation did Brigitte McMahon win the inaugural women's triathlon?
7. In what sport did triple Olympic champion Alexander Karelin (RUS) lose for the first time in 13 years?
8. María Isabel Urrutia's victory in weightlifting made her the first ever Olympic champion from which South American nation?
9. Name the only British woman to claim an athletics title in Sydney.
10. In terms of the number of gold medals won, what was Great Britain's most successful sport at these Games?

Answers on page 208

39

Athens 2004

1. Which city held Olympic events for the first time in over 1600 years when it staged the men's and women's shot put competitions in its ancient stadium?
2. Events in which sport were held in the Panathenaic Stadium, the main venue for the Athens Games of 1896?
3. In what track event did Liu Xiang become China's first ever male champion in Olympic athletics?
4. Which male African runner completed the first 1500-5000m double at the Olympics since 1924?
5. After representing her native Jamaica in six previous Olympics, veteran sprinter Merlene Ottey now competed in her seventh in the colours of what former Yugoslav republic?
6. Which South American nation celebrated its first ever Olympic titles after taking two golds in tennis?
7. Gal Fridman became what Middle Eastern country's first ever Olympic champion when taking gold in windsurfing?
8. Name the 17-year-old who became Britain's youngest medallist in Athens when taking a silver in boxing.
9. Which nation pulled off a surprise semi-final victory over hot favourites the United States on its way to winning the men's basketball title?
10. In what sport did a Greek pairing win a shock gold after only being allowed to compete because the host nation received an automatic qualifying spot?

Answers on page 208

Beijing 2008

Part 1

1. Which North American city was defeated by Beijing in the final round of voting in the bid election to host these Games?
2. China's Li Ning, who lit the cauldron at the opening ceremony after being hoisted high into the air with cables, had won three Olympic titles in what sport in 1984?
3. What nicknames were given to the Olympic stadium and the aquatic centre in Beijing?
4. Which separate member of the IOC staged the equestrian events for these Games?
5. South Africa's Natalie du Toit, whose left leg was amputated following a road accident, took part in which sport to become the first female amputee to compete at a Summer Olympics?
6. In athletics, name either of the Ethiopian runners who completed a 5000-10000m double at these Games.
7. Which African nation gained its first ever Olympic medal when Ismail Ahmed Ismail took silver in the men's 800m?
8. What track event was added to the women's athletics programme and won in world record time by Russia's Gulnara Samitova-Galkina?
9. Name the female star who broke her own world record when retaining the women's pole vault title.
10. Which American sprinter gained a bronze medal in both the men's 100 and 200 metres?

Answers on page 209

Beijing 2008

Part 2

1. In which sport did an American 'Redeem Team' compete successfully in Beijing?
2. The unofficial title of 'the world's strongest man' went to a competitor from which European country after he had won the super-heavyweight (+105kg) weightlifting event?
3. Georgeta Andrunache of Romania took her fifth Olympic gold in what sport?
4. Ryoka Tamura-Tani of Japan became the first competitor to win five medals in the same individual event at the Summer Olympics when she took a silver in which sport?
5. Which nation claimed both the silver and bronze medals in the men's beach volleyball competition?
6. What serious disease did Dutch swimmer Maarten van der Weijden recover from to win gold in the 10km open water marathon?
7. Russia's Buvaisa Satiyev claimed his third Olympic title in which sport?
8. Name the boxer who won Great Britain's 19th and last gold medal of these Games.
9. What nation won the most medals in Beijing?
10. Which veteran British guitarist performed at the closing ceremony as part of the handover of the Games from Beijing to London?

Answers on page 209

London 2012

Part 1 – The Build-up

1. Which city did London defeat in the final round of voting in the bid election to host the 2012 Olympics?
2. In which country was the bid election held?
3. Shortly after selecting London as the host city, the IOC voted to drop which two ball sports from the 2012 Games?
4. In August 2009, the IOC approved the introduction of which sport for women at the 2012 Olympics?
5. Name the Conservative politician who was appointed Minister for Sport and Olympics in May 2010.
6. Who became the first person to qualify for Team GB for London 2012 after reclaiming a world swimming title in summer 2011?
7. In October 2011, who was appointed head coach of the Great Britain women's Olympic football team, with Stuart Pearce taking the men's role?
8. In May 2012, which British Olympic champion ran the first leg of the Olympic torch relay from Land's End, when the torch began its journey around the UK?
9. Recorded by Muse and released in June 2012, what was the title of the official song of the London Olympics?
10. In July 2012, which private security company became embroiled in a scandal over its failure to provide enough security staff for the London Games?

Answers on page 210

London 2012

Part 2 – The Games

1. Competition began on 25 July 2012, two days before the opening ceremony, when Great Britain took on New Zealand in a women's football match played in which city?
2. Which Oscar-winning British film director was the artistic director of the opening ceremony?
3. How many young athletes lit the cauldron in the Olympic Stadium in the climax to the opening ceremony?
4. The preliminary rounds and quarter-finals of which sport took place in the Copper Box in the Olympic Park?
5. What venue in Buckinghamshire staged the rowing competition and the canoe sprint events?
6. In athletics, who broke his own world record when claiming the men's 800m title?
7. Who completed a thrilling 5000-10000m double on the athletics track?
8. How many medals did Michael Phelps did win in London to become not only the most successful competitor here but also the most decorated Olympian of all time?
9. Name the British woman who made history in London by becoming the first female Olympic boxing champion.
10. What collective name was given to the 70,000 unpaid volunteers who played a vital role in ensuring the success of London 2012?

Answers on page 210

2. SUMMER OLYMPIC SPORTS

Archery

1. What is the name of the bow used in Olympic archery?
2. What colour is the bull's-eye on an archery target?
3. The most successful archer in Olympic history, Hubert van Innis gained nine medals competing for which European nation?
4. What was the surname of the British siblings who both won archery medals at the the 1908 London Games?
5. Sharing his name with a famous American film composer, which 18-year-old US Army private won the men's individual title when archery was reintroduced to the Olympics in 1972?
6. Name the American who in 1984 regained the men's individual title he had first won in 1976.
7. What European nation placed third in the men's team event in both 1988 and 1992?
8. Which South Korean archer scored a bull's-eye with her final shot to snatch the women's individual title in 2004?
9. What famous sporting venue staged the archery events at London 2012?
10. Which European country prevented a South Korean 'clean sweep' of all four titles in London by taking the men's team event?
11. Name the South Korean woman who was the most successful archer at London 2012 with two golds.
12. What nation has won four silver medals but no golds in the history of the women's team event?

Answers on page 211

Athletics

Part 1 – Men's track events
1. Which Briton won gold in two track events at the 1900 Games, only to died from pleurisy the following year aged 27?
2. The original 'Flying Finn', which distance runner took three gold medals and set two world records at the 1912 Games?
3. Name the British 400m runner who gained four Olympic medals in the 1920s and later pioneered the filming of athletics.
4. In 1948, Arthur Wint became what country's first Olympic champion in any sport when claiming the 400m title?
5. Who became the first German male to win an Olympic track title when taking 100m gold at the 1960 Rome Games?
6. Which track event at the 1976 Montreal Olympics was won in world record time by Sweden's Anders Garderud?
7. Finland's Martti Vainio was disqualified for a doping offence after placing second in what event at the 1984 Games?
8. Name the African sprinter who gained four Olympic silver medals, but no golds, in the 1990s.
9. Who ran the anchor leg when Great Britain pulled off a shock victory over the USA in the men's 4x100 final at Athens 2004?
10. Which Bahraini athlete was disqualified for a drug offence after finishing first in the men's 1500m in Beijing?
11. What Caribbean nation won its first ever Olympic gold in men's athletics when taking a relay title at London 2012?
12. At the age of 34, who regained the 400m hurdles title he had first won in 2004, becoming both the oldest athletics champion in London and the oldest winner of this event?

Answers on page 211

Athletics

Part 2 – Women's track events

1. Which ill-fated Japanese athlete was runner-up in the inaugural Olympic 800m for women in 1928?
2. Name the Australian runner who won four Olympic golds in four different events between 1956 and 1964.
3. In 1972, which defending champion failed to reach the final of her event after mistaking the finishing line in her semi-final and placing fifth? And which British athlete benefited from her blunder to finish fourth and qualify for the final, where she set a British record that lasted nearly seven years?
4. Which legendary athlete claimed her seventh Olympic medal when taking 400m gold in world record time in 1976?
5. In 1984, the inaugural women's 400m hurdles final was won by a competitor from what African country?
6. Who became China's first Olympic champion in an athletics track event when she took the inaugural 5000m title in 1996?
7. In 2000, which African athlete regained the 10000m title she had first won in 1992?
8. Which Caribbean country won women's 4x100m gold in 2000, the only time it has claimed this title?
9. What track event was won in 2004 by Yulia Nesterenko of Belarus?
10. After finishing runner-up at 200m in both 2004 and 2008, which American star finally secured this title at London 2012 and added two more wins in the relays for a golden treble?
11. Which nation achieved a 1-2 in the women's 1500m in 2012?
12. Name the Australian star who won the 100m hurdles in Olympic record time at London 2012.

Answers on page 212

Athletics

Part 3 – Men's field events

1. Clarence Houser (USA) retained his Olympic title in which field event in 1928?
2. What was the nickname of theology professor Bob Richards (USA), twice Olympic pole vault champion in the 1950s?
3. Which American shot putter retained his Olympic title in 1956 and gave his name to a throwing technique in this event?
4. The world record was broken five times in which men's field event at the 1968 Mexico Games?
5. Yuri Sedykh of the Soviet Union won two Olympic gold medals and one silver in which field event?
6. Which American shot putter went from serving coffee in the Olympic village in Atlanta in 1996 to earning a silver medal four years later in Sydney?
7. In what field event at Sydney 2000 did the USA's men fail to win a medal for the first time in Olympic history (excluding the boycotted Games of 1980)?
8. For which European nation did Virgilijus Alekna take gold in the discus in both 2004 and 2008.
9. Which Norwegian star retained the men's javelin title in 2008?
10. Name the Polish field eventer who was the first athletics champion at both Beijing 2008 and London 2012.
11. Keshorn Walcott became the first ever field event champion from which Caribbean country when successful in the javelin at London 2012?
12. Who won the long jump in London to give Great Britain its first gold in this event since 1964?

Answers on page 212

Athletics

Part 4 – Women's field events

1. In which field event did British female athletes win five consecutive Olympic silver medals from 1936 onwards?
2. Which female Soviet athlete earned three medals in field events at the 1952 Olympics?
3. When competing in her fifth Olympics in 1968, Lia Manoliu of Romania finally won a gold medal in what field event?
4. Which 16-year-old West German was Olympic high jump champion in 1972 and repeated her triumph 12 years later?
5. Name the British javelin thrower who gained two Olympic medals in the 1980s.
6. In 1996, Ukraine's Inessa Kravets became the first Olympic champion in what field event?
7. Which American star won the inaugural women's pole vault title at the 2000 Sydney Olympics?
8. Poland's Kamila Skolimowska became the first Olympic champion in what event after its introduction in 2000?
9. Name the Russian athlete who earned four Olympic medals in the horizontal jumps between 2004 and 2008, including gold in the long jump in Athens.
10. With victory in the high jump at Beijing 2008, Tia Hellebaut made history as the first female Olympic champion in athletics for which European nation?
11. At London 2012, which New Zealander retained her shot put crown from Beijing after she was promoted to gold after the original winner, Nadzeya Ostapchuk of Belarus, was stripped of the title for failing a drug test?
12. Sandra Perković won which field event at London 2012 to become Croatia's first ever Olympic champion in athletics?

Answers on page 213

Athletics

Part 5 – Marathons, walks and combined events (men)

1. Runners from which country claimed the Olympic marathon title in both 1932 and 1948?
2. What long distance event was won by Britons Tommy Green in 1932 and Harold Whitlock in 1936?
3. Rafer Johnson and CK Yang, who finished 1-2 after a thrilling duel in the 1960 Olympic decathlon, were training partners at which California university?
4. Name the Munich-born winner of the 1972 Olympic marathon.
5. Wladimir Cierpinski, who retained the Olympic marathon title in 1980, represented which nation?
6. Jefferson Perez, the 1996 Olympic champion in the 20km walk, competed for what South American country?
7. Erki Nool won the decathlon title in 2000 representing which Baltic state?
8. Now competing for Canada, who placed fourth for Great Britain in the men's marathon in both 2000 and 2004?
9. Name the Polish race walker who completed a hat-trick of Olympic 50km walk titles in 2004.
10. In which event did Cuba's Leonel Suárez win Olympic bronze in both 2008 and 2012?
11. At London 2012, Erick Barrondo's silver in the 20km race walk gave which Central American nation its first ever Olympic medal in any sport?
12. The last gold medallist in athletics at London 2012, Stephen Kiprotich's victory in the men's marathon made him only the second ever Olympic champion from which African country?

Answers on page 213

Athletics

Part 6 – Marathons, walks and combined events (women)

1. Name the two British athletes who finished in the top four in the first Olympic pentathlon for women in 1964.
2. What was the last event of an Olympic pentathlon?
3. Which nation completed a clean sweep of the pentathlon medals at Montreal 1976?
4. Name the reigning World champion who was runner-up in the inaugural Olympic marathon for women in 1984.
5. Which American star set a world record when winning heptathlon gold in 1988 and easily retained her title in 1992?
6. Chen Yueling became China's first ever Olympic champion in athletics when successful in what event at Barcelona 1992?
7. Athletes from which Asian country won the women's marathon in both 2000 and 2004?
8. Which British athlete, who announced her retirement from athletics in May 2012, earned a bronze in the heptathlon at Athens 2004?
9. In 2008, who originally finished second in the heptathlon but was later disqualified after testing positive for a banned drug?
10. Which long distance event did Russia's Elena Lashmanova win in world record time at London 2012?
11. Tiki Gelana set an Olympic record when winning the women's marathon in 2012 for which African country?
12. Which German multi-eventer was a distant runner-up to Britain's Jessica Ennis in the 2012 heptathlon?

Answers on page 214

Badminton

1. When taking the women's singles title in 1992, Susi Susanti became the first ever Olympic champion in any sport for which Asian country?
2. What nationality was the only non-Asian badminton medallist at the 1996 Atlanta Olympics?
3. Also in 1996, which Chinese world champion made a shock exit at the quarter-final stage of the women's singles?
4. Mia Audina, who was runner-up for Indonesia in the women's singles in 1996, later married a gospel singer and represented what European nation in 2000?
5. Who partnered Joanne Goode as Great Britain earned a bronze medal in the mixed doubles in 2000?
6. Which 'wild man' of Indonesian badminton redeemed his reputation by winning the men's singles in 2004?
7. Name the British pair who gained a silver medal in the mixed doubles in 2004.
8. Which Chinese player claimed the women's singles title in both 2004 and 2008?
9. Name the flamboyant player threw his shoes and racket into the crowd after taking gold in the men's singles in 2008?
10. Also in Beijing, Markis Kido and Hendra Setiawan won the men's doubles representing which south-east Asian country?
11. At London 2012, which European nation finished a distant second in the medal table behind China, who collected all five golds on offer?
12. Saina Nehwal's bronze in the women's singles in 2012 made her only the second ever female Olympic medallist from which Asian country?

Answers on page 214

Basketball

Part 1 (1936–1980)

1. Which team were runners-up to the USA in the inaugural Olympic basketball final of 1936?
2. The medals at these Games were awarded by the Canadian-American sports coach who invented basketball. What is his name?
3. A member of the victorious USA team of 1948, how did Don Barksdale make history when appearing at the Games?
4. What Middle Eastern nation lost all five matches at the 1948 Olympics, twice being defeated by 100 points?
5. In 1952, American referee Vince Farrell had to be carried from the court after being attacked by fans and players of which South American team?
6. The victorious USA team of 1956 were led by Bill Russell and KC Jones, who both later enjoyed outstanding careers in the NBA with which team?
7. What South American nation took a bronze in basketball at both the 1960 and 1964 Games?
8. Which East European country pulled off shock victories over the Soviet Union in the semi-finals of both the 1968 and 1976 men's tournaments?
9. Who scored the winning basket in the epic 1972 final – but died only six years later aged 26?
10. Which country won the first two titles in women's Olympic basketball?
11. What Soviet bloc nation claimed a silver medal in the women's competition in 1980?
12. Which fellow European nation did Yugoslavia overcome in the 1980 men's final?

Answers on page 215

53

Basketball

Part 2 (1984–2012)

1. Name the future legend of the sport who averaged 17.1 points per game to help the USA claim the men's title in 1984.
2. Which US star won four golds between 1984 and 2000 and was the first female player to compete at five Olympics?
3. Lynette Woodward, who helped the USA win the 1984 women's title, later became the first female player for which famous basketball team?
4. For what nation did Oscar Schmidt score an Olympic record of 55 points in a preliminary round defeat by Spain in 1988?
5. At the 1992 Olympics, which member of the American 'Dream Team' had the highest points-per-game average?
6. Name the San Antonio Spurs centre who scored 28 points to help the USA defeat Yugoslavia in the 1996 men's final.
7. Which female US centre scored a national record of 35 points against Japan in the 1996 semi-finals and went on to win the first of four Olympic gold medals?
8. What European nation lost by only two points to the USA in the men's semi-finals in 2000?
9. In 2004, which nation became the first to defeat the USA men's team since the introduction of professional players 12 years earlier?
10. In 2008, what country was runner-up in the women's final for the third time in a row?
11. Name the USA player who scored 30 points to lead his team to victory over Spain in the men's final at London 2012.
12. Which European country won its first ever medal in women's Olympic basketball when taking a silver in 2012?

Answers on page 215

Boxing

Part 1 (1904–1980)

1. What unique feat in Olympic boxing history was achieved by Oliver Kirk (USA) at the inaugural tournament of 1904?
2. The oldest Olympic boxing champion, Great Britain's Richard Gunn won which weight category in 1908 at the age of 37?
3. At what weight did Ronald Rawson win Olympic gold for Britain in 1920?
4. Which British middleweight of the 1920s was the first man to retain an Olympic boxing title and ended his amateur career unbeaten in over 300 bouts?
5. What South American country claimed both featherweight titles in the 1930s?
6. Bronze medallist at flyweight in 1936, Louis Lauria (USA) was the first winner of which trophy, awarded to the Olympic boxer with the best style and technique?
7. Name either of the weight categories that were added to the boxing schedule for the 1952 Olympics.
8. Britain's Terry Spinks, who died in April 2012 aged 74, was Olympic champion in what weight division in 1956?
9. Name the British fighter who defeated Soviet fighter Aleksei Kiselyov to claim the middleweight title in 1968.
10. Which Olympic heavyweight champion of the 1960s went on to win 76 of his professional 81 fights and was nicknamed the 'Heywood Giant'?
11. Light flyweight champion in 1972 and a competitor until 1980, which Hungarian was the first boxer to fight at four Olympics?
12. Which middleweight champion from Montreal 1976 later turned professional and became world heavyweight champion?

Answers on page 216

Boxing

Part 2 (1984–2012)

1. Hot favourite to win heavyweight gold in 1984, which future world champion had to settle for bronze after being controversially disqualified in his semi-final bout?
2. For what country did Lennox Lewis win Olympic gold at Seoul in 1988?
3. Name the future legend of the sport who took lightweight gold at the 1992 Barcelona Games.
4. Which future world heavyweight champion claimed the Olympic super-heavy title in 1996?
5. Name the Cuban heavyweight who won his third Olympic title in 2000, becoming only the third boxer to achieve this feat.
6. The 20-year-old Kazakh boxer Bekzat Sattarkhanov was killed in a car crash in December 2000, only three months after being crowned Olympic champion in what weight division?
7. Which Cuban boxer retained his lightweight title in 2004 by defeating Britain's Amir Khan and two years later was hired to coach the Great Britain Olympic boxing team?
8. Which British boxer was sent home from the 2008 Games because he failed to meet the weight limit for his division?
9. Who won Ireland's only gold medal of London 2012 by taking the inaugural women's lightweight title?
10. Name the Hull boxer whose triumph in London made him Britain's first Olympic bantamweight champion since 1908.
11. Ryōta Murata won Japan's only boxing gold in 2012 when successful in which weight division?
12. Welsh boxer Fred Evans took silver in 2012 after losing the welterweight final to an opponent from which country?

Answers on page 216

Canoeing

1. What is the shortest distance for events in Olympic sprint canoeing following changes made for London 2012?
2. What French term is used for the second-chance round in Olympic canoeing?
3. In which event at the 1948 Games did Czechoslovakia's Jan Brzák-Felix retain a title from 1936?
4. Karen Hoff became the first female Olympic canoeing champion in 1948 when competing for which European nation?
5. Name the Swedish sprint canoeist who won six Olympic gold medals between 1948 and 1960 and was head coach of the Swedish team at the 1964 Games.
6. Which East European country completed a clean sweep of all four slalom titles in 1972 after visiting the Olympic course the previous year and building an exact replica of it to train on?
7. Ian Ferguson, who claimed four canoeing titles between 1984 and 1992, is what nation's most successful Olympian?
8. Which European country took three golds in the men's 1000m kayak fours between 1988 and 2004?
9. Michal Martikan, winner of the Canadian slalom singles title in 1996, was the first Olympic champion to represent what newly independent European nation?
10. Name the British kayaker who won three Olympic medals in the period 2000–2008, including K-1 1000m gold in Beijing.
11. In canoeing at London 2012, the inaugural men's K-1 200m event was won by which British kayaker?
12. French slalom canoeist Tony Estanguet claimed his third Olympic title in which event in 2012?

Answers on page 217

Cycling

Part 1 (1896–1988)

1. Paul Masson, the winner of three cycling titles at the 1896 Athens Olympics, competed for which nation?
2. Which European nation claimed its fourth consecutive 4000m team pursuit gold at Los Angeles in 1932?
3. Which legendary British cyclist recovered from serious war wounds to earn two silver medals at the 1948 London Games?
4. In 1952, what European country retained its Olympic team road race title and achieved a 1-2 in the individual road race?
5. At the 1960 Rome Games, which Italian rider became the only cyclist in Olympic history to win both the time trial and match sprint events?
6. Name the future legend of the sport who placed 12th in the Olympic road race in 1964.
7. Which French police officer won five cycling medals, including three golds, in the period 1964–76?
8. At the 1976 Montreal Olympics, which European team was banned from using its one-piece silk suits because of the unfair aerodynamic advantage they would give?
9. What was the only event held when women's cycling was introduced to the Olympics in 1984?
10. A men's team from what country indulged in 'blood boosting' techniques (not illegal at the time) at Los Angeles in 1984?
11. Dan Frost took victory in the individual points race in 1988 for which European country?
12. In which decade in this period was Olympic track cycling first held indoors?

Answers on page 217

Cycling

Part 2 (1992–2012)

1. Name the unemployed carpenter from Merseyside who won Britain's first Olympic gold in cycling for 72 years when successful in the men's individual pursuit in 1992.
2. Which multiple Tour de France champion claimed the individual road race title at the 1996 Games?
3. Which Italian rider won the inaugural women's mountain bike title in 1996 (cross country) and repeated her triumph in 2000?
4. Name the former winner of the Tour de France who won the individual road race event at the 2000 Olympics.
5. Which female Dutch cyclist earned six medals, including four golds, in the period 2000–2004?
6. In what event at the 2004 Athens Games did Britain's Chris Hoy take the first gold of his Olympic career?
7. Which Briton was favourite to win the first women's BMX title in 2008 but finished last after crashing in the final round?
8. In track cycling, who did Rebecca Romero defeat in an all-British final of the women's individual pursuit in Beijing?
9. Name the British rider who place third in the men's time trial at London 2012 as team-mate Bradley Wiggins won gold.
10. Which six-race event was added to the track cycling programme for London 2012, Britain's Laura Trott winning the inaugural women's competition?
11. Which venue in Essex staged the men's and women's mountain biking events of the 2012 Games?
12. Which Latvian rider lived up to his nickname of 'The Machine' by retaining his men's BMX title in 2012?

Answers on page 218

Diving

1. In which decade was an Olympic diving competition first held?
2. How many competitors take part in an individual final in Olympic diving?
3. Which country claimed 10 consecutive men's springboard diving titles between 1920 and 1968?
4. Which female US diver gained four Olympic gold medals in the 1950s?
5. Name the Italian diver who secured three successive men's 10m platform titles between 1968 and 1976.
6. In 1988, which American star recovered from hitting the springboard with his head (causing a wound that required stitches) to successfully defend his two titles and become the first male diver to complete an Olympic 'double double'?
7. How old was China's Fu Mingxia when she won the first of her two women's 10m platform crowns in 1992?
8. Chantelle Newbery's victory in the women's platform in 2004 gave what country its first Olympic diving title in 80 years?
9. Alexandre Despatie was runner-up in the men's springboard event in 2004 and 2008 representing which nation?
10. Name the Australian diver whose victory in the men's 10m platform event in 2008 denied China a clean sweep of all eight Olympic diving titles.
11. Which Chinese diver became the first woman to win three consecutive Olympic titles in diving with victory at London 2012 in the springboard synchronised event?
12. Name the male American diver who gained two medals at London 2012.

Answers on page 218

Equestrian

Part 1 (1900–1976)

1. The first modern Olympic champion in equestrian, Aimé Haegman, represented which European nation when successful in show jumping in 1900?

2. Charles Pahud de Mortanges, who claimed four Olympic golds in three-day eventing in the period 1924–32, competed for what European country?

3. In which competition did Great Britain take its only equestrian medal of the 1936 Berlin Games?

4. Which European team finished first in the dressage in 1948 but was later disqualified because one of its members was, contrary to the rules of the time, not a fully commissioned military officer?

5. In 1956, who became Britain's first female Olympic medallist in equestrian as GB took bronze in the team jumping?

6. Name the famous Italian rider who claimed the individual jumping title at the 1960 Rome Games.

7. Which South American nation won its only Olympic medal in equestrian in 1964?

8. In 1968, who became Britain's first female Olympic champion in equestrian as part of the successful three-day event team?

9. What horse helped two riders win three-day event team golds (1968, 1972) and appeared in two films in the 1970s?

10. In 1972, which 45-year-old West German rider became the first female equestrian to win an individual Olympic event?

11. Name the male West German rider who won the 1976 individual jumping title without incurring any faults.

12. On which horse owned by the Queen did Princess Anne (now the Princess Royal) compete for Britain at the 1976 Games?

Answers on page 219

Equestrian

Part 2 (1980–2012)

1. Which now-defunct nation won its second and last team dressage title in 1980?
2. Name the outstanding New Zealand equestrian who retained his individual three-day crown in 1988.
3. Which male West German rider ended his illustrious Olympic career in 1988 after winning a record six gold medals?
4. Name the horse on which Germany's Isabell Werth gained four gold and two silver medals in the period 1992–2000.
5. Which southern hemisphere nation achieved a 1-2 in the individual eventing at the 1996 Atlanta Games?
6. In 2000, which Australian man became the first rider to win three golds in the three-day team event?
7. Name the female German rider who originally placed first in the individual three-day event at the 2004 Athens Games but was demoted to ninth place after a penalty infraction.
8. In 2008, which female Dutch equestrian claimed her third consecutive Olympic title in the individual dressage?
9. Which female British equestrian earned two bronze medals at the Beijing Olympics?
10. Name the male German equestrian who won gold at London 2012 to become the first rider to hold Olympic, World and European titles in individual eventing at the same time.
11. Competing in his sixth Olympics in 2012, which 54-year-old rider helped Great Britain claim the team jumping title for the first time since 1952?
12. Name the horse that Britain's Charlotte Dujardin rode to victory in the individual and team dressage events in 2012.

Answers on page 219

Fencing

1. How many rounds, and of what duration, does an Olympic fencing match have?
2. What word of French origin is used to denote a fence-off to decide tied matches?
3. Which legendary Italian fencer won five golds at the 1920 Olympics, setting a record that remains unequalled.
4. Ellen Osier, who the claimed the women's title in 1924 without losing a bout, competed for which European country?
5. What European nation won every men's team sabre title between 1928 and 1960?
6. Name the French star who retained his individual foil title at the 1956 Melbourne Games, taking the fourth and final title of an outstanding Olympic career.
7. What nation gained three consecutive women's team foil gold medals between 1968 and 1976?
8. In 1992, Eric Srecki won the men's individual épée title representing what country?
9. When claiming the women's individual sabre gold in 2004, Mariel Zagunis became the first competitor in 100 years to win a fencing title for which nation?
10. Name the female Italian star who in 2008 became the first fencer in Olympic history to claim three consecutive individual foil titles, and then in 2012 won team gold to take her overall Olympic tally to six golds and nine medals in total.
11. Which German fencer took gold in the women's individual épée in 2008 and silver in 2012?
12. Rubén Limardo's victory in the men's individual épée at London 2012 provided which South American nation with only its second gold medal in Olympic history?

Answers on page 220

Football

Part 1 (1900–1968)

1. How many players aged over 23 are allowed in an Olympic football squad?
2. Held in 1900, the inaugural Olympic football tournament was won by which amateur club from the East End of London?
3. Which European nation gained three successive bronze medals in football in the period 1908–1920?
4. What North African country placed fourth at the 1928 Olympics despite losing its last two matches 6–0 and 11–3?
5. Great Britain exited the 1936 tournament at the quarter-final stage after losing 5–4 to which East European nation?
6. After leading Sweden to Olympic gold in 1948, a trio of forwards turned professional and joined which top European club?
7. What nation's shock second-round exit from the 1952 tournament was not reported by its national press for several months?
8. Name the famous player who set his team on course for gold by scoring the opening goal of the 1952 final.
9. Which south-east Asian country placed fourth in the 1956 tournament, still its highest finish in Olympic football?
10. In 1960, which European nation qualified for the semi-finals on the toss of a coin and went on to win the tournament?
11. What Asian country took a surprise bronze medal in the 1968 football tournament?
12. How many players were sent off in the 1968 final, in which Hungary retained their Olympic title with a 4–1 defeat of Bulgaria?

Answers on page 220

Football

Part 2 (1972–2012)

1. Which future Manchester City player scored both of Poland's goals in their 2–1 win over Hungary in the 1972 final?
2. Who helped Brazil gain a silver medal in 1984 and went on to captain and manage his national side and coach the Brazil Olympic team?
3. Which southern African country finished fifth in the 1988 Olympic tournament after defeating Italy 4–0 in a preliminary round match?
4. Name the Atlético Madrid striker whose last-minute goal gave Spain a thrilling victory in the 1992 final.
5. Who did the United States defeat in the inaugural women's final at the 1996 Atlanta Games?
6. Which African team defeated Spain on penalties in the men's final of 2000?
7. Which current Premier League striker was the leading goalscorer at the 2004 men's tournament, his eight goals helping his country win their first Olympic football title?
8. Name the female American striker who retired in 2004 after helping her country take two Olympic golds.
9. In 2008, which nation earned a silver medal in the men's tournament and a bronze in the women's?
10. Who missed a spot-kick as Great Britain's men lost on penalties to South Korea in the quarter-finals at London 2012?
11. Which team knocked out Great Britain at the quarter-final stage of the 2012 women's tournament and then lost a thrilling semi-final to the USA?
12. Name the Mexican striker who scored twice as his country upset Brazil to win the men's final at London 2012.

Answers on page 221

Gymnastics

Part 1 – Men's events

1. In which decade did men first compete in Olympic gymnastics?
2. The first gymnastics gold medal was awarded in a team event won by which European country?
3. In 1912, Italy's Albero Braglia became the first gymnast to retain which Olympic title?
4. Who gained six medals for Yugoslavia in the period 1924–36 and appeared at the opening ceremony of the 1996 Olympics at the age of 97?
5. Name the Soviet star who won three golds in 1956 to end his Olympic career with a highly impressive total of 11 medals.
6. What country claimed four successive men's team combined titles between 1960 and 1976?
7. Which Japanese gymnast took silver in the all-around competition in 1976 to end his Olympic career with a total of 12 medals, including eight golds?
8. Name the Soviet gymnast who in 1980 earned eight medals, including three golds, and became the first male gymnast in Olympic history to be awarded a perfect 10 score.
9. Which competitor for the Unified Team won six gold medals at Barcelona 1992?
10. Which Chinese gymnast was the star performer in Beijing after taking three golds, including two in individual events.
11. Name the Japanese star won three medals at London 2012, including the individual all-around title.
12. On which apparatus did two British artistic gymnasts win individual medals in 2012.

Answers on page 221

Gymnastics

Part 2 – Women's events

1. In what decade did women first compete in Olympic gymnastics?
2. Which East European nation claimed its only women's team title at the 1948 London Games?
3. Name the Soviet gymnast who earned seven medals in 1952, still a record haul for a female competitor at a single Olympics.
4. Agnes Keleti took five golds in the 1950s for which European country?
5. Which charismatic and hugely popular Czech gymnast collected seven Olympic golds in the 1960s.
6. In 1976, which Soviet star became the first woman in Olympic history to achieve perfect 10 scores on both the vault and in the floor exercise?
7. Name the female Romanian gymnast who won four golds at the 1984 Olympics.
8. Shannon Miller of the United States claimed the Olympic title on which apparatus in 1996?
9. What East European country retained its team combined exercises title in 2004?
10. Which nation secured its fourth consecutive women's rhythmic group all-around title at London 2012?
11. Nicknamed the 'Flying Squirrel', which female US artistic gymnast won gold in both the individual and team all-around events at London 2012?
12. On which apparatus did Britain's Beth Tweddle win bronze in 2012 to become the first British female gymnast to earn an individual Olympic medal?

Answers on page 222

Handball

1. Which European nation was runner-up to Germany in the inaugural men's Olympic handball competition in 1936?
2. Which now-defunct nation took Olympic gold in both 1972 and 1984?
3. In what decade was a women's tournament first held at the Olympics?
4. Name the winners of the first two women's titles.
5. In 1980, what Middle Eastern country suffered a record 44–10 defeat to Yugoslavia in the men's event?
6. Name the male Russian goalkeeper who won a record three golds – representing a different team each time – between 1988 and 2000.
7. Which Asian team retained its women's title at the 1992 Barcelona Olympics?
8. What Scandinavian country completed a hat-trick of women's titles in 2004?
9. Which North European nation was runner-up to France in the men's competition of 2008?
10. What venue staged the semi-finals and finals of the handball tournament at London 2012?
11. France retained their men's title in 2012 with a narrow victory over which European team?
12. Which Balkan county won its first medal in Olympic history when runner-up to Norway in the women's handball competition at London 2012?

Answers on page 222

Hockey

1. Which European team claimed the first two Summer Olympic hockey titles?
2. What Asian country remained unbeaten in Olympic hockey between 1928 and 1956, winning all six titles in this period?
3. In 1972, what nation became the first from outside Asia to win an Olympic hockey title?
4. All eleven players from which team were banned for life by the IOC for disruptive behaviour at the 1972 Games which included pouring water on the head of the president of the International Hockey Federation?
5. In 1980, what nation won the inaugural women's tournament despite selecting its squad only a week before the Games started?
6. Who was the goalkeeper for Great Britain's men's team at both the 1984 and 1988 Olympics?
7. In 1988, which player scored twice as Great Britain defeated West Germany in a memorable men's final?
8. What was the most successful Asian country in the men's tournament in both 1996 and 2000?
9. What southern hemisphere nation claimed its first ever hockey medal when runner-up in the women's tournament in 2000?
10. Which country won its first Olympic title in the men's hockey in 2004?
11. At London 2012, Britain gained its first Olympic medal in hockey in 20 years with a defeat of which team in the women's bronze medal match?
12. Which nation successfully defended its men's crown in 2012, a win they celebrated with a 'wild boat party' on the Thames?

Answers on page 223

Judo

1. What nationality was the first Olympic judo champion?
2. Which European nation claimed the first two titles in the men's open category (no weight limit)?
3. What name is given to the deciding period in Olympic judo if a bout ends in a tie after the normal duration of five minutes?
4. Name the British male judoka who won two Olympic silver medals in the 1980s.
5. Austria's Peter Seisenbacher retained his Olympic title in which weight division in 1988?
6. Who became Britain's most successful female judoka after earning Olympic medals in 1992 and 2000?
7. With victory in the extra-lightweight (-60kg) class in 2004, which Japanese competitor became the first judoka to win three consecutive Olympic titles?
8. When taking light heavyweight gold in 2008, Naidangiin Tüvshinbayar became the first Olympic champion in any sport for which Asian country?
9. What nation claimed three women's judo titles at the 2008 Olympics?
10. In which weight division did Kim Jae-Bum of South Korea win silver in 2008 and gold in 2012?
11. Nicknamed 'Teddy Bear', which French judoka claimed the men's heavyweight title at London 2012?
12. Which London-born female judoka was runner-up in the half-heavyweight category (78 kg) in 2012, earning Britain its first medal in the sport since 2000?

Answers on page 223

Modern Pentathlon

1. The freestyle swimming event of the modern pentathlon is held over how many metres?
2. Which European nation provided the top four finishers in the first Olympic modern pentathlon in 1912?
3. Who became the first non-military winner of the individual event in 1952 and retained his title four years later.
4. What East European nation claimed two individual and two team titles in the 1960s?
5. The victorious Great Britain trio in the 1976 team event comprised Adrian Parker, Danny Nightingale, and who else?
6. Which Soviet modern pentathlete concluded his outstanding Olympic career in 1980 by winning team gold at the age of 37 and taking a record seventh medal in total?
7. Which East European country won the last men's team competition in 1992?
8. What nation won three successive men's titles between 2000 and 2008?
9. At Beijing 2008, which discipline in the modern pentathlon was held at the Ying Tung Natatorium?
10. The 2012 London Games saw which two disciplines combined for the first time?
11. Name the Czech winner of the men's title at London 2012.
12. What is the only country to have won a medal in each of the four women's competitions held since 2000?

Answers on page 224

Rowing

Part 1 (1900–1976)

1. A trio of brothers, the Goslers, helped which nation take gold in the coxed fours in 1900?
2. On which river were the rowing events held at both the 1900 and 1924 Games?
3. Name the British rower who gained medals at five successive Olympics between 1920 and 1936.
4. What country claimed a remarkable eight consecutive Eights titles between 1920 and 1956?
5. Teams from which Cambridge University college won the coxless fours for Great Britain in both 1924 and 1928?
6. Which British rower won two titles on one day at the 1932 Olympics and served in World War II as an RAF squadron leader, once saving his own life by rowing four miles through a minefield in a dinghy after his plane crashed in the Atlantic?
7. Name the British rower who emulated his father by claiming gold at the 1948 Olympics.
8. What South American country earned its only rowing title in Olympic history at the 1952 Games?
9. Name the Soviet rower who won his third consecutive single sculls gold in 1964.
10. Which southern hemisphere nation gained its only Eights title at the 1972 Munich Games?
11. Over what distance did female rowers compete when women's rowing was added to the Olympic schedule in 1976?
12. In 1976, brothers Frank and Alf Hansen won gold in the double sculls for which European country?

Answers on page 224

Rowing

Part 2 (1980–2012)

1. What East European nation claimed its fourth successive Fours title in 1980?
2. Name the Finnish rower who won his third consecutive gold in the single sculls in 1984.
3. Since 1988, both men and women have competed over a course measuring how many metres?
4. What nation retained its men's fours title in 1996 but has not been successful in this event since then?
5. Which European country collected four consecutive women's quadruple sculls titles between 1992 and 2004?
6. In 2004, which Romanian woman became first rower to compete in six Olympics, the oldest rower to win a gold medal and the oldest competitor in an endurance sport to win gold?
7. In both 2004 and 2008, the women's double sculls title was won by Georgina and Caroline Evers-Swindell, a pair of identical twin sisters from what country?
8. Which East European country claimed its third consecutive women's coxless pairs title in 2008?
9. Who partnered Mark Hunter as Great Britain took gold in the men's lightweight double sculls in 2008 and silver in 2012?
10. Which men's title did Great Britain win for the fourth time in a row in 2012?
11. Name the female British rower who ended a run of three successive Olympic silver medals by taking gold at London 2012.
12. What nation took its only gold in rowing at London 2012 when retaining the women's eights title?

Answers on page 225

73

Sailing

Part 1 (1900–1984)

1. Give either of the two main reasons why sailing at the 1900 regatta should not, in the eyes of some sports historians, be counted as an official Olympic event.
2. What was the surname of the British husband and wife who won gold in the 7 metre class in 1920?
3. Which Baltic port staged the sailing events at both the 1936 and 1972 Olympics?
4. Name the Danish sailor who won four consecutive gold medals between 1948 and 1960.
5. In which now-discontinued class (named after a bird) did Great Britain claim its only sailing title of the 1948 Games?
6. What southern hemisphere country won the Flying Dutchman class in 1956 and 1964?
7. In 1964, a pairing from which Caribbean nation took gold in the Star class?
8. Name the British sailor who retained his Olympic title at the Munich Games of 1972.
9. Which of the North American Great Lakes staged the sailing events at the 1976 Montreal Olympics?
10. In 1980, Esko Rechardt secured the Olympic Monotype title for what Scandinavian country?
11. All 13 members of which nation's sailing team earned gold or silver medals at the 1984 Games?
12. Name the New Zealander who won the Finn class in 1984 and skippered *Black Magic I* to victory in the 1995 America's Cup.

Answers on page 225

Sailing

Part 2 (1988–2012)

1. Which now-defunct nation won its last Olympic sailing gold at the 1988 Seoul Games?
2. Name either of the boat classes that were introduced to women's Olympic sailing in 1992.
3. What nationality is Theresa Zabell Lucas, Olympic champion in the 470 class in both 1992 and 1996?
4. In which class did Britain's Ben Ainslie win his first Olympic gold medal in 2000?
5. In 2004, which Brazilian sailor reclaimed the Laser title he had first won in 1996?
6. In what class did 'Three blondes in a boat' win gold for Great Britain in both 2004 and 2008?
7. Name the British duo who won gold in the Star class in 2008 and silver in 2012.
8. Which British sailor triumphed in the men's Laser class at Beijing 2008 but could only place seventh in 2012 after suffering a back injury during competition?
9. Which English county staged the sailing events at the 2012 London Games?
10. What was the only Open class (i.e. open to both men and women) in 2012?
11. Which class was added to the women's programme for 2012 and won by a trio from Spain?
12. What nation topped the medal table for sailing in 2012?

Answers on page 226

Shooting

1. In which decade were shooting events first staged at the Olympics?
2. What nation won five of the seven military rifle team competitions held between 1900 and 1920?
3. Known as 'The mecca of rifle shooting', what venue staged the shooting events at the 1948 London Games?
4. In 1968, which Scarborough vet was crowned Britain's first individual Olympic champion in shooting in 44 years?
5. Linda Thom represented which nation when winning the sports pistol event in 1984?
6. Which British marksman retained his small bore rifle title at the 1988 Seoul Olympics.
7. Name the British shooter who took gold in the men's double trap in 2000 after beating the defending champion, Russell Mark of Australia, in a shoot-off.
8. In 2004, Italy's Andrea Bennelli became the first female champion in a mixed Olympic shooting event when she claimed what title?
9. Competing in the men's small-bore rifle – three positions, which American shooter twice lost gold with his final shot, throwing away his lead in 2004 when hitting an opponent's target and then misfiring and missing his own target in 2008?
10. Which Czech shooter won gold in 2008 after equalling the world record with a perfect 400 score in the women's 10 metre air pistol competition?
11. In which event did Peter Wilson win gold for Britain in 2012?
12. What Asian country topped the medal table in shooting at London 2012?

Answers on page 226

Swimming

Part 1 – Men's events

1. Which European country provided the winners of the first two Olympic men's 100m freestyle titles?
2. Name the British swimmer who gained five Olympic medals between 1908 and 1920.
3. What nation took five of the six men's swimming titles at the Los Angeles Games of 1932?
4. Known as the 'Seaweed Streak' for his vegetarian diet, which Australian teenager claimed three titles at the 1956 Olympics?
5. In 1964, which American became the first swimmer to win four gold medals at the same Games?
6. The winner of the men's 200m and 400m individual medley titles in 1972 represented which European nation?
7. Which Soviet swimmer became the first man to break 15 minutes for 1500m when taking gold at the 1980 Games?
8. The first man to swim 100 metres in less than 49 seconds, which American swimmer amassed eight Olympic gold medals between 1984 and 1992?
9. Name the Russian star who retained both his Olympic 50m and 100m freestyle titles at the 1996 Atlanta Games.
10. What nationality was the winner of the men's 100 and 200m breaststroke titles at both the 2004 and 2008 Olympics?
11. Name either of the individual events that Michael Phelps won for the third consecutive time at London 2012.
12. Name the Chinese winner of both the men's 400 and 1500m freestyle titles in 2012.

Answers on page 227

Swimming

Part 2 – Women's events

1. In 1912, which Australian swimmer became the sport's first female Olympic champion with victory in the 100m freestyle?
2. Name the British teenager who won 100m backstroke gold in world record time at the 1956 Melbourne Olympics.
3. Which Australian female swimmer claimed three consecutive Olympic 100m freestyle titles between 1956 and 1964?
4. In the 1970s, which US Olympic swimmer became known as 'Surly Shirley' because of her public accusations of drug cheating by her East German rivals?
5. In 1984, which women's individual final saw the first dead-heat in Olympic swimming history, the American pair of Carrie Steinstiefer and Nancy Hogshead both winning gold?
6. Name the East German swimmer who won six golds (a record for a woman in any sport) at the 1988 Seoul Games.
7. Which Irish swimmer claimed three Olympic titles in 1996 but later received a four-year ban for a drugs-related offence?
8. Which female Dutch swimmer was nicknamed 'Invincible Inky' after winning three Olympic golds in 2000?
9. In what event did Great Britain's Rebecca Adlington break the world record when striking gold in Beijing?
10. British pair Keri-Anne Payne and Cassie Patten took silver and bronze, respectively, in what swimming event in 2008?
11. Which 17-year-old American starlet won four golds at London 2012, including the 100 and 200m backstroke titles?
12. Name the 15-year Chinese swimmer who claimed the 200 and 400m individual medley titles in London, setting a controversial world record in the longer event.

Answers on page 227

Synchronised Swimming

1. In what decade was synchronised swimming introduced as a medal sport at the Olympics?
2. What nation took gold in the duet in 1988 and was runner-up in both 1984 and 1992?
3. What was the surname of the American twin sisters who won silver in the duet in 1988 and gold in 1992?
4. After representing the Unified Team in 1992, Anna Kozlova earned two bronze medals competing for what nation in 2004?
5. Controversy flared before the 1996 Games after a duet team had its choice of free routine vetoed as inappropriate. A duet from which European country had planned to base their routine on the fate of Jewish women at a Nazi concentration camp?
6. How did the Russian duet of Olga Brushnika and Marija Kiselyeva make Olympic history in 2000?
7. Which Asian country was runner-up in both the team and duet competitions in 2004?
8. En route to winning a third consecutive gold in the team event in 2008, Russia scored a perfect 50 points in the free routine when performing to 'Living Sea', a musical piece based on the theme from which series of fantasy adventure films?
9. Which North African country placed eighth in the team final at Beijing 2008 and seventh at London 2012?
10. Name the European nation that won two minor medals in both 2008 and 2012.
11. What was the venue for the synchronized swimming at London 2012?
12. Twenty-four pairs took part in the duet competition in London, with how many advancing to the final after a preliminary round?

Answers on page 228

Table Tennis

1. In what decade was table tennis first included as a medal sport at the Olympics?
2. Automatic qualification for singles events at the Olympics is given to the top ranked how many players in the world?
3. What European nation claimed a bronze medal in the men's doubles at the 1988 Seoul Games?
4. Which Asian country claimed the inaugural women's doubles title in 1988?
5. What European country provided the men's singles champion of 1992?
6. Name the diminutive Chinese player who retained her singles and doubles titles in 1996.
7. What European country claimed a bronze medal in the men's doubles at Sydney 2000?
8. Which special administrative region of China took silver in the men's doubles in 2004?
9. What was the only European country to win a table tennis medal in Beijing?
10. Name the Polish female Paralympic champion who competed in table tennis at both the 2008 and 2012 Olympics, reaching the last 32 of the women's singles in London.
11. What was the venue for table tennis at London 2012?
12. In 2012, China won all four titles for the second Games in a row, but which other Asian country picked up two bronze medals?

Answers on page 228

Taekwondo

1. In which decade was taekwondo first staged as a demonstration sport at the Summer Olympics?
2. Men and women are each allowed to compete in how many weight categories at the Olympics?
3. Women's taekwondo matches comprise three rounds, each lasting how many minutes?
4. Tran Hieo Ngan's flyweight bronze in 2000 made him the first ever Olympic medallist for which south-east Asian country?
5. Name the American winner of the men's flyweight title in 2000 and the welterweight title in 2004.
6. China's Chen Zhong retained which women's title in 2004?
7. Hadi Saei won 68 kg gold in 2004 and 80 kg gold in 2008 representing which Middle Eastern country?
8. Which Asian country claimed its third consecutive men's heavyweight title in 2008?
9. Rohullah Nikpai gained a bronze at flyweight (58 kg) in 2008 to become the first ever Olympic medallist in any sport for what central Asian republic?
10. Name the Welsh teenager who won a surprise gold in the women's lightweight category (-57 kg) at London 2012 to become Britain's first Olympic champion in taekwondo.
11. In 2012, who earned a bronze medal in the middleweight division (80 kg) after being controversially selected for Team GB instead of World No 1 Aaron Cook?
12. Which Central African nation celebrated its first ever Olympic medal after Anthony Obame took silver in the heavyweight category (+80 kg) at London 2012?

Answers on page 229

Tennis

Part 1 – Men's events

1. Which French player won a record six Olympic medals, including four golds, between 1900 and 1920?
2. One of the fabled 'Four Musketeers', which French star won two silver medals at the 1924 Paris Games?
3. Who won the men's singles title when tennis was reintroduced to the Olympics in 1988?
4. Which American world No 1 and top seed was beaten in the third round of the men's singles in 1992?
5. Name the Spanish runner-up in the 1996 men's singles tournament.
6. What nation took its only medal in Olympic tennis history when claiming the men's doubles title in 2000?
7. Name the South American player who won two golds in Athens in 2004.
8. Which big name did Lu Yen-Hsun of Taiwan knock out of the men's singles at the Beijing Olympics?
9. Which South American player was runner-up to Rafa Nadal in the 2008 men's singles final?
10. In a men's singles semi-final match at London 2012, who did Switzerland's Roger Federer defeat in the longest match in Olympic tennis history?
11. Who did Britain's Andy Murray beat in his singles semi-final before dispatching Roger Federer in three straight sets in the gold medal match?
12. The men's doubles final saw No 1 seeds Bob and Mike Bryan (USA) defeat a pairing from which European country?

Answers on page 229

Tennis

Part 2 – Women's events

1. Which seven-time Wimbledon singles champion gained her only Olympic singles title at the 1908 London Games?
2. Which British woman won a record five Olympic medals (and two Wimbledon singles titles) in the 1920s?
3. Nicknamed 'Little Miss Poker Face' for her unchanging expression, which American star claimed the women's singles crown at the 1924 Paris Games?
4. At the 1984 Olympics, which future great won the women's demonstration tournament despite being only 15 years old?
5. Which American pairing with the same surname (but not related) retained their women's doubles title in 1996?
6. Name the European player who lost to Lyndsey Davenport (USA) in three sets in the 1996 singles final.
7. In 2004, what country knocked out defending champions the USA in the first round of the women's doubles and went on to claim a surprise title?
8. At Sydney 2000, who became the first player in 76 years to win two tennis golds at the same Olympics?
9. Which fellow Russian did Elena Dementieva defeat in the women's singles final of 2008?
10. Whose reign as the World No 1 ranked women's player lasted only one week in August 2008 after she lost in the quarter-finals of the Olympic singles?
11. Who did Serena Williams (USA) trounce 6–0 6–1 in the women's singles gold medal match at London 2012?
12. Reintroduced in 2012, the mixed doubles saw Britain's Laura Robson and Andy Murray defeated in the gold medal match by a pairing from which East European country?

Answers on page 230

Triathlon

1. How many metres do competitors swim in the triathlon?
2. The event concludes with a run over what distance?
3. Which French world champion could only place seventh in the inaugural Olympic men's competition at Sydney 2000?
4. Simon Whitfield won gold in 2000 and bronze in 2008 competing for which country?
5. In 2004, what nation filled the first two places in the men's competition?
6. Name the Briton who placed sixth in the women's event at Athens 2004, the best Olympic performance by a British triathlete of either gender until Helen Jenkins placed fifth at London 2012.
7. Which future British world champion finished twelfth in the men's competition in 2008?
8. Jan Frodeno, the 2008 men's champion, competes for what European nation?
9. Competitors from which country earned gold and bronze medals in the women's event in 2008?
10. At London 2012, the swimming part of the triathlon was held in which recreational lake in Hyde Park?
11. The 2012 women's event ended in dramatic style, with a photo-finish needed to separate a pair of athletes from which two European nations?
12. Team GB's Brownlee bothers, Alistair and Jonathan, won gold and bronze medals, respectively, in the men's event at London 2012, with silver going to a rival from which other European country?

Answers on page 230

Volleyball

1. If needed, the fifth set in an Olympic volleyball match is played to how many points?
2. What is the name of the skilled defensive player who is not allowed to serve and is distinguished by a different coloured vest?
3. What East European nation pulled off a surprise win over the Soviet Union in the men's final of 1976?
4. Name the European country that won bronze in the men's event in 1996 and gold in 2000.
5. What country won the inaugural women's competition in 1964 to the delight of local fans?
6. Which South American nation gained its only Olympic volleyball medal when taking silver in the 1988 women's tournament?
7. What country claimed its third consecutive women's volleyball title in 2000?
8. What was the famous venue for the beach volleyball events at the 2000 Olympics?
9. Which nation won the men's volleyball title in 2004 and the women's title in 2008?
10. What venue in central London staged the beach volleyball competition in 2012?
11. The women's beach volleyball final at London 2012 was contested by two pairs from what nation?
12. In men's volleyball, which country recovered from a two-set deficit to win the gold medal match in 2012?

Answers on page 231

Water Polo

1. In which decade was water polo first included in the Olympics?
2. What European country won the first four men's titles?
3. Which fellow East European nation was runner-up to Hungary in the 1964 tournament?
4. Both the 1936 and 1984 titles were decided by what method after two teams finished level on points in the medal round?
5. Which country did Italy defeat in overtime in the all-European final of 1992?
6. In 2000, Russia's men recorded the highest score in Olympic history when beating which East European team 21–5?
7. Name the winners of the inaugural women's title in 2000.
8. Which European nation claimed its third consecutive men's title in 2008?
9. What West European country claimed the women's title in Beijing?
10. Which former Yugoslav republic defeated Italy in the men's final at London 2012?
11. Which country won its first women's title with victory over Spain in 2012?
12. How many nations have competed in the women's tournament at each of the last three Olympics?

Answers on page 231

Weightlifting

1. The highest weight category for women is for competitors weighing over how many kilograms?
2. Viggo Jensen, who became the first Olympic weightlifting champion in 1896, represented which European country?
3. Tommy Kono won two weightlifting gold medals in the 1950s for what nation?
4. Name the Soviet star who won two Olympic super-heavyweight titles in the 1970s and set 79 world records.
5. Which East European nation's weightlifting team withdrew from the 1988 Games after two of its lifters were stripped of their gold medals for failing a drug test?
6. Greece's Pyrros Dimas claimed three successive golds in what weight category between 1992 and 2000?
7. Which Bulgarian-born lifter secured his third consecutive Olympic featherweight crown for Turkey in 1996?
8. Iran's Hossein Rezah Zadi retained his Olympic title in what category in 2004?
9. Which country won seven medals – but no golds – in weightlifting at Beijing 2008?
10. What was the venue for the weightlifting competition at London 2012?
11. Featured in a BBC TV documentary, *Girl Power: Going For Gold*, in the run-up to 2012, which female lifter set a British record on her way to 12th place in the women's 58kg event?
12. Which central Asian republic claimed four weightlifting titles at London 2012?

Answers on page 232

Wrestling

1. Since 2008, an Olympic freestyle wrestling match has comprised how many periods of two minutes?
2. Which now-defunct nation has won the most Olympic wrestling titles?
3. What European country has gained 17 medals in Olympic wrestling but won its last one over a century ago?
4. Carl Westergren, the first weightlifter to claim three Olympic titles, competed for which European nation?
5. In 1968, Daniel Robin earned silver medals in both the freestyle and Greco-Roman disciplines when representing what country?
6. What was the surname of the Soviet twin brothers who both won Olympic freestyle titles in the 1980s?
7. Iryna Merleni of Ukraine became the first female Olympic wrestling champion when taking which freestyle title in 2004?
8. Name the only non-Asian country to claim a women's title at the Beijing Games.
9. In 2008, which Swedish wrestler originally won bronze in the 84kg class but was disqualified by the IOC after he protested at the officiating during the medal ceremony?
10. Mijaín Lopez, who retained the men's 120kg Greco-Roman title at London 2012, competes for what Caribbean nation?
11. Name the Uzbeki wrestler who in 2012 secured a third consecutive victory in the men's 120kg freestyle division.
12. Japanese wrestlers claimed three of the four women's freestyle titles in 2012. Which nation won the other one?

Answers on page 232

Discontinued Sports

1. Events in which outdoor sport at the 1900 Olympics were attended by only one paying spectator?
2. Which sport only appeared at the 1900 Games and was won by a touring team from England?
3. What sport was only held in 1904 and 1908, both titles going to Canada?
4. Which indoor sport made its sole Olympic appearance in 1908 and saw American Jay Gould take the only title on offer?
5. The final of which sport at the 1908 Games saw a contest between two police teams, City of London Police defeating their colleagues from the Liverpool force?
6. What sport of Basque origin was only held as a medal sport at the 1900 Games but later reappeared three times as a demonstration sport?
7. In what team sport did Daniel Carroll win gold medals for two different countries in the early 20th century?
8. Name the winners of a record three baseball titles.
9. Which country claimed the baseball title at the 2008 Beijing Games?
10. Name the winning nation in women's softball in Beijing.
11. What country claimed a record three softball titles?
12. Argentina are the reigning Olympic champions in which discontinued sport, having won the last tournament in 1936?

Answers on page 233

3. SUMMER OLYMPICS NUMBERS

Part 1 – A Question of Age

1. The youngest known medallist and competitor in Olympic history, how old was Greece's Dimitrios Loundras when he took a team bronze in gymnastics in 1896?
   (a) 10
   (b) 11
   (c) 12
   (d) 13

2. The oldest female Olympic champion, how old was Britain's Sybil ('Queenie') Newell when she won archery gold in 1908?
   (a) 51
   (b) 53
   (c) 55
   (d) 57

3. Britain's oldest Olympic champion, what age was Joshua ('Jerry') Millner when he claimed a shooting title in 1908?
   (a) 59
   (b) 61
   (c) 63
   (d) 65

4. Great Britain's youngest Olympic champion, how old was Isabella Moore when she won a swimming relay gold in 1912?
   (a) 14
   (b) 15
   (c) 16
   (d) 17

Answers on page 234

5. The oldest ever Olympian, Sweden's Oscar Swahn was what age when he earned a team silver medal in shooting in 1920?
   (a) 60
   (b) 64
   (c) 68
   (d) 72

6. The youngest male individual Olympic champion, how old was Japan's Kusuo Kitamura when he took gold in swimming at the 1932 Los Angeles Games?
   (a) 12
   (b) 13
   (c) 14
   (d) 15

7. The youngest individual champion at the Summer Olympics, how old was Marjorie Gestring (USA) when she won gold in the women's 3m springboard diving event in 1936?
   (a) 11
   (b) 12
   (c) 13
   (d) 14

8. The oldest medallist in Olympic athletics, what age was Great Britain's Terrence ('Tebbs') Lloyd Johnson when he took bronze in the 50km walk in 1948?
   (a) 44
   (b) 46
   (c) 48
   (d) 50

Answers on page 234

9. The oldest female competitor in Olympic history, how old was British equestrian Lorna Johnstone when she took part in dressage at the 1972 Munich Games?
(a) 60
(b) 63
(c) 67
(d) 70

10. The oldest competitor at London 2012, what age was the Japanese equestrian Hiroshi Hoketsu when he placed 40th in the individual dressage event?
(a) 65
(b) 67
(c) 69
(d) 71

11. What is the minimum age requirement for horses competing in the equestrian events?
(a) 5
(b) 6
(c) 7
(d) 8

12. Olympic boxers must be within what age range?
(a) 16–30
(b) 17–34
(c) 18–35
(d) 19–40

Answers on page 234

93

Part 2 – How many?

1. Competitors from how many nations took part in the first modern Olympics at Athens in 1896?
   (a) 14
   (b) 16
   (c) 18
   (d) 20

2. How many sports were contested in 1896?
   (a) 6
   (b) 9
   (c) 12
   (d) 15

3. How many gold medals did Great Britain win at the 1908 London Olympics?
   (a) 36
   (b) 46
   (c) 56
   (d) 66

4. Uganda's John Akii-Bua, the 1972 Olympic 400m hurdles champion, had how many brothers and sisters?
   (a) 12
   (b) 22
   (c) 32
   (d) 42

Answers on page 234

5. How many gold medals did the Soviet Union win at the 1980 Moscow Olympics?
   (a) 50
   (b) 60
   (c) 70
   (d) 80

6. Great Britain won the same number of gold medals at each of the four Summer Olympics between 1980 and 1992. How many did they win at each Games?
   (a) 3
   (b) 4
   (c) 5
   (d) 6

7. How many gold medals did Australia win at the Sydney Games of 2000?
   (a) 16
   (b) 20
   (c) 24
   (d) 28

8. The Olympic Cauldron at London 2012 comprised how many copper petals, each one representing a national team competing at the Games?
   (a) 200
   (b) 202
   (c) 204
   (d) 206

Answers on page 234

9. How many sports were contested at London 2012?
   (a) 26
   (b) 28
   (c) 30
   (d) 32

10. The largest team in 2012, Team GB was made up of how many athletes?
    (a) 501
    (b) 521
    (c) 541
    (d) 561

11. How many world records were set at London 2012?
    (a) 28
    (b) 32
    (c) 36
    (d) 40

12. The United States topped the medal table in London after winning 46 golds and how many medals in total?
    (a) 102
    (b) 104
    (c) 106
    (d) 108

Answers on page 234

Part 3 – Name the Year

1. The Ancient Olympic Games began in 776 BC and continued until which year when they were abolished by a decree of Emperor Theodosius?
   (a) 93 AD
   (b) 193 AD
   (c) 293 AD
   (d) 393 AD

2. At which year's Summer Olympics did the number of competitors exceed 10,000 for the first time?
   (a) 1988
   (b) 1992
   (c) 1996
   (d) 2000

3. In which year did the number of *female* competitors at a Summer Games exceed 1,000 for the first time?
   (a) 1960
   (b) 1964
   (c) 1968
   (d) 1972

4. In athletics, in which year was the women's 400 metres first run at the Olympics?
   (a) 1960
   (b) 1964
   (c) 1968
   (d) 1972

Answers on page 235

5. In boxing, in which year were bronze medals first awarded for both losing semi-finalists?
   (a) 1936
   (b) 1948
   (c) 1952
   (d) 1956

6. In what year was a women's cycling event first held?
   (a) 1980
   (b) 1984
   (c) 1988
   (d) 1992

7. In which year were equestrian events first held at the Olympics?
   (a) 1900
   (b) 1904
   (c) 1908
   (d) 1912

8. In what year did a Great Britain football team last win Olympic gold?
   (a) 1900
   (b) 1908
   (c) 1912
   (d) 1920

Answers on page 235

9. In which year did women first compete in Olympic judo?
   (a) 1980
   (b) 1984
   (c) 1988
   (d) 1992

10. In athletics, in what year did a non-Kenyan athlete last win the men's 3000m steeplechase?
    (a) 1980
    (b) 1984
    (c) 1988
    (d) 1992

11. What was the last Olympics at which no world records were set in athletics?
    (a) 1988
    (b) 1992
    (c) 1996
    (d) 2000

12. In what year was London awarded the 2012 Olympics?
    (a) 2004
    (b) 2005
    (c) 2006
    (d) 2007

Answers on page 235

Part 4 – Placings and scores

1. What is the highest placing by a British woman in an Olympic marathon?
   (a) 4th
   (b) 6th
   (c) 8th
   (d) 10th

2. What is the best finish by a British man in an Olympic hammer competition?
   (a) 3rd
   (b) 5th
   (c) 7th
   (d) 9th

3. By what score did the USA beat Canada in the inaugural basketball final in 1936?
   (a) 19–8
   (b) 49–38
   (c) 79–68
   (d) 109–98

4. In what position did Emil Zatopek finish when failing to defend his marathon title in 1956?
   (a) 4th
   (b) 6th
   (c) 8th
   (d) 10th

Answers on page 235

5. Where did Bulgaria place in the medal table at the 1980 Moscow Olympics?
   (a) 3rd
   (b) 6th
   (c) 9th
   (d) 12th

6. By what score did Great Britain beat West Germany in the 1988 men's hockey final?
   (a) 2–0
   (b) 2–1
   (c) 3–1
   (d) 3–2

7. By what score did Nigeria beat Argentina in the 1996 men's football final?
   (a) 2–0
   (b) 2–1
   (c) 3–1
   (d) 3–2

8. By what score did the United States win the women's football finals of 1996, 2004 and 2012?
   (a) 1–0
   (b) 2–1
   (c) 2–0
   (d) 3–1

Answers on page 235

9. By what score did the Netherlands beat Great Britain in the men's hockey bronze medal match at London 2012?
   (a) 6–2
   (b) 7–2
   (c) 8–2
   (d) 9–2

10. In what position did Australia finish in the medal table at London 2012?
    (a) 10th
    (b) 12th
    (c) 14th
    (d) 16th

11. Team GB suffered its biggest defeat in men's volleyball at London 2012 when losing by what score to France?
    (a) 32–15
    (b) 36–15
    (c) 40–15
    (d) 44–15

12. What position was Team GB's highest placed finisher in the men's marathon at London 2012?
    (a) 20th
    (b) 30th
    (c) 40th
    (d) 50th

Answers on page 235

Part 5 – A Matter of Time

1. The world's longest ever wrestling match took place at the Stockholm Olympics of 1912. How long did it last?
   (a) 5 hrs 40 mins
   (b) 7 hrs 40 mins
   (c) 9 hrs 40 mins
   (d) 11 hrs 40 mins

2. At Berlin in 1936, Jesse Owens equalled the Olympic record for the 100 metres in athletics when taking gold in what time?
   (a) 10.1 secs
   (b) 10.2
   (c) 10.3
   (d) 10.4

3. What was the world record time set by Australia's Herb Elliott when he won the 1500m in athletics at the 1960 Rome Games?
   (a) 3 mins 35.6 secs
   (b) 3:37.6
   (c) 3:39.6
   (d) 3:41.6

4. By how much time did Ethiopia's Abebe Bikila win the marathon at the 1964 Tokyo Olympics?
   (a) 1 min 8 secs
   (b) 2 mins 8 secs
   (c) 3 mins 8 secs
   (d) 4 mins 8 secs

Answers on page 236

5. In swimming, Valdimir Salnikov (USSR) claimed the men's 1500m freestyle title in 1980 in what world record time?
(a) 14 mins 48.27 secs
(b) 14:58.27
(c) 15:08.27
(d) 15:18.27

6. In rowing, by how many seconds did Great Britain win the men's eights final at Sydney 2000?
(a) 0.80
(b) 1.80
(c) 2.80
(d) 3.80

7. What was the world record-equalling time set by China's Liu Xiang when he won 110m hurdles gold at Athens in 2004?
(a) 12.81 secs
(b) 12.91
(c) 13.01
(d) 13.11

8. What was the world record time set by Usain Bolt when he claimed the 200m title in athletics at Beijing 2008?
(a) 19.10 secs
(b) 19.20
(c) 19.30
(d) 19.40

Answers on page 236

9. In cycling, by how many seconds did Team GB's Bradley
   Wiggins win the men's time trial at London 2012?
   (a) 6
   (b) 10
   (c) 14
   (d) 18

10. In what world record time did the USA win gold in the
    women's 4x100m in athletics at London 2012?
    (a) 38.82 secs
    (b) 39.82
    (c) 40.82
    (d) 41.82

11. What was the world record time set by Kenyan athlete David
    Rudisha when he won 800m gold in 2012?
    (a) 1 min 39.91 secs
    (b) 1:40.91
    (c) 1:41.91
    (d) 1:42.91

12. Mo Farah won 10000m gold in London in 27 mins 30.42 secs,
    but what time did GB team-mate Alistair Brownlee record for
    the same distance in the triathlon after a 1500m swim and
    a 43km bike ride?
    (a) 29 mins 07 secs
    (b) 30:07
    (c) 31:07
    (d) 32:07

Answers on page 236

Part 6 – Weights and Measures

1. How far did Bob Beamon leap when he set a stunning world record in the long jump at the 1968 Mexico Games?
   (a) 8.60m
   (b) 8.70m
   (c) 8.80m
   (d) 8.90m

2. Set by Kenny Harrison (USA) when he won gold in 1996, what is the Olympic record in the men's triple jump?
   (a) 17.89m
   (b) 17.99m
   (c) 18.09m
   (d) 18.19m

3. How tall is Japan's Mizuki Noguchi, winner of the 2004 women's marathon?
   (a) 1.50m
   (b) 1.60m
   (c) 1.70m
   (d) 1.80m

4. The heaviest female competitor in Olympic history, how much did Ukrainian weightlifter Olha Korobka weigh when runner-up in the +75 kg category at Beijing 2008?
   (a) 147 kg
   (b) 157 kg
   (c) 167 kg
   (d) 177 kg

Answers on page 236

5. What was the world record height cleared by Russia's Yelena Isinbayeva when she retained her pole vault title in 2008?
   (a) 5.05m
   (b) 5.10m
   (c) 5.15m
   (d) 5.20m

6. How tall is the tallest ever Olympian, the Chinese basketball player Yao Ming, who appeared at his last Games in 2008?
   (a) 2.09m
   (b) 2.19m
   (c) 2.29m
   (d) 2.39m

7. The lowest weight category in Olympic men's weightlifting is for competitors weighing up to how many kilograms?
   (a) 50 kg
   (b) 56 kg
   (c) 60 kg
   (d) 66 kg

8. What was the Olympic record distance thrown by Tatyana Lysenko (RUS) when she won the women's hammer competition at London 2012?
   (a) 72.18m
   (b) 74.18m
   (c) 76.18m
   (d) 78.18m

Answers on page 236

9. Women's boxing was introduced at London 2012, with the heaviest weight class being middleweight. What is the permitted weight range in this class?
   (a) 55–60 kg
   (b) 61–68 kg
   (c) 69–75 kg
   (d) 76–81 kg

10. Gymnast Rebecca Tunney was both the youngest and shortest member of Team GB at London 2012. She was 15 years old and how tall?
   (a) 1.45m
   (b) 1.50m
   (c) 1.55m
   (d) 1.60m

11. What weight were the medals awarded at London 2012?
   (a) 175–200g
   (b) 275–300g
   (c) 375–400g
   (d) 475–500g

12. The heaviest competitor in Olympic history, how much did Guam's Ricardo Blas Jr weigh when he took part in judo in 2012?
   (a) 188 kg
   (b) 198 kg
   (c) 208 kg
   (d) 218 kg

Answers on page 236

4. SUMMER OLYMPICS MIXED BAG

First Things First

Part 1 (1896–1976)

1. Francis Lane (USA) became the first person to win an event at the modern Olympics when he won the first heat of which athletics competition at the 1896 Games?
2. Charles Bennett made history as Great Britain's first Olympic champion in athletics with victory in what event in 1900?
3. William DeHart Hubbard (USA) became the first black competitor to win an individual Olympic gold medal when successful in which athletics event in 1924?
4. Which aquatic sport made its Olympic debut in 1936?
5. Nina Romashkova took the Soviet Union's first ever Olympic gold medal when winning what athletics event in 1952?
6. Which British Olympic champion of the 1960s was the first female flag bearer for Great Britain at a Summer Olympics opening ceremony and also the first woman to win the BBC Sports Personality of the Year award?
7. Ghana's Clement ('Ike') Quartey became the first black African Olympic medallist when taking silver in which sport in 1960?
8. The 1968 Mexico Olympics saw the first drug disqualification when a Swedish modern pentathlete tested positive for an excessive amount of what illegal substance?
9. At the 1976 Montreal Games, who became the first gymnast in modern Olympic history to receive a perfect 10 score?
10. Excluding the 1906 Interim Games, which American athlete was the first sprinter to retain an individual Olympic title?

Answers on page 237

First Things First

Part 2 (1980–2008)

1. In this period, who became the first President of the United States to officially open a Summer Olympics?
2. Competing while seated in a wheelchair, Neroni Fairhall of New Zealand became both the first Paralympian and the first paraplegic to compete at an Olympics when she took part in what sport at the 1984 Los Angeles Games?
3. In 1988, fencer Kerstin Palm became the first woman to compete at seven Olympic Games. Which country did she represent?
4. Anthony Nesty, who made history in 1988 as the first black Olympic swimming champion, represented which South American nation?
5. What southern African nation made its Olympic debut at Barcelona 1992 and won two medals in athletics?
6. Yael Arad took a silver medal in judo in 1992 to become the first ever Olympic medallist for which Middle Eastern country?
7. In 2000, Marla Runyan (USA) became the first legally blind person to compete at the Olympics, reaching the final of which track event in athletics?
8. In what combat sport were women allowed to compete for the first time at the 2004 Athens Games?
9. Which Asian country won its first ever individual Olympic gold when Abhinav Bindra claimed a title in shooting in 2008?
10. Which Central American nation celebrated its first Olympic title after Irving Saladino won the men's long jump in 2008?

Answers on page 237

First Things First

Part 3 – London 2012

1. China's Yi Siling won the first gold medal at London 2012 when successful in which sport?
2. Name the Yorkshire woman who secured Great Britain's first medal of the Games with a silver in road cycling.
3. Who became both the first double amputee and the first male Paralympian to compete at the Olympics when contesting the 400 metres in athletics?
4. Sixteen-year-old Wojdan Shaherkani made history as the first woman from Saudi Arabia to compete in an Olympic Games when she took part in which sport?
5. Who took gold in the men's 400m in athletics to become Grenada's first Olympic medallist in any sport?
6. In 2012, Steve Grotowski and John Garcia-Thompson became Britain's first Olympic competitors in which sport?
7. Which southern African nation won its first Olympic medal when Nijel Amos took silver in the men's 800m in athletics?
8. Pavlos Kontides's silver in sailing's Laser class made him the first Olympic medallist from which Mediterranean country?
9. With victory in the women's 200m backstroke, 15-year-old Plymouth schoolgirl Ruta Meilutyte became the first Olympic medallist in swimming for which European country?
10. Nicknamed 'Captain Canada' for his longevity and achievements, which equestrian made history in 2012 as the first competitor in any sport to take part in 10 Olympics?

Answers on page 238

Controversy

Part 1 (1908–1980)

1. Which athletics final at the 1908 Games featured the only 'walkover' in Olympic history, Britain's Wyndham Halswelle running alone to win gold after the original final had been declared void and a re-run ordered?
2. Which legendary runner travelled to the 1932 Los Angeles Games but was declared a professional (by the athletics governing body, the IAAF) and banned from competing?
3. At the 1936 Berlin Olympics, in which sport did Germany's Toni Merkens win gold after being fined rather than disqualified for obstruction when competing in his first race?
4. Gymnastics official Marie Provaznikova defected at the 1948 Games, saying "there is no freedom of speech" in her home country. What European country was she from?
5. Teams from which two nations clashed in the infamous 'Blood in the Water' water polo match at the 1956 Olympics?
6. At the 1964 Tokyo Games, which Australian swimmer was arrested after allegedly stealing a 'souvenir' flag from the entrance to the Emperor's palace?
7. The medal ceremony for the men's 200 metres at the 1968 Mexico Olympics featured a highly controversial 'Black Power' salute involving which two US athletes?
8. What two countries clashed in "the most controversial game in international basketball history" at the 1972 Games?
9. Name the Soviet modern pentathlete who was disqualified for cheating in the fencing event at the 1976 Olympics.
10. After winning which athletics field event in 1980 did Poland's Wladyslaw Kozakiewicz respond to the jeering Soviet crowds with an obscene bent elbow gesture?

Answers on page 238

Controversy

Part 2 (1984–2012)

1. At Los Angeles in 1984, which athletics event did American idol Mary Decker crash out of after tangling with Zola Budd?
2. Name the British star who appeared at a press conference at the 1984 Games wearing a T-shirt with the slogan, 'Is the world's second greatest athlete gay?'.
3. At Seoul 1988, which American boxer was scandalously denied a gold medal in the light middleweight division after dominating his Korean opponent?
4. In 1992, members of which men's volleyball team shaved their heads in protest at a controversial defeat in their first match?
5. Which female athletics star won five medals at Sydney 2000 but was stripped of them after admitting in 2007 that she had taken performance enhancing drugs?
6. Name either of the Greek athletes who were banned for faking a motorcycle accident to avoid a drugs test at Athens 2004.
7. In diving at the 2008 Olympics, who sparked a row with partner Tom Daley in the 10m synchronised event by talking on his mobile phone during the final?
8. Angel Matos of Cuba was banned for life from which indoor sport after assaulting a referee at the Beijing Games?
9. On the first day of women's football at London 2012, which team walked off the pitch in protest when the wrong flag was displayed to introduce their players, causing the kick-off of their match to be delayed by over an hour?
10. In which sport at London 2012 were eight players expelled from a competition by the world governing body for 'not using one's best efforts to win a match' and 'conducting oneself in a manner that is clearly abusive or detrimental to the sport'?

Answers on page 239

Family Ties

Part 1 (1900–1960s)

1. British brothers Reggie and Laurie Doherty claimed an Olympic title in which sport at the 1900 Paris Games?

2. In 1908, British husband and wife Charles and Frances Rivett-Carnac became the first British married couple to win Olympic gold medals when they triumphed in what sport?

3. The fathers of actress Grace Kelly and actor and comedian Hugh Laurie were both Olympic champions in which sport?

4. The father of which famous British actress won gold in athletics at the 1936 Olympics and lived until the age of 100?

5. What relation were Paul and Hilary Smart (USA), winners of the Star class sailing event at the 1948 London Games?

6. British runner Bill Nankeville, who placed sixth in the 1500m final in 1948, is the father of which well known comedian and impressionist?

7. Three Swedish brothers, the Nordahls, helped their country win Olympic gold in what sport in 1948?

8. Distance runner Emil Zatopek famously won three gold medals at the 1952 Olympics in Helsinki, but in what athletics event at the same Games did his wife Dana also take gold?

9. What was the surname of the burly Russian sisters who claimed a total of five Olympic titles in athletics between 1960 and 1964, only to disappear from the sporting scene after sex tests were introduced to their sport in 1966?

10. Competitors in athletics, who are the only British mother and daughter to have won Olympic medals?

Answers on page 239

Family Ties

1. The first British sisters to compete at a Summer Olympics, which sport did Jane Bullen and Jennifer Loriston-Clarke (née Bullen) take part in between 1968 and 1988?
2. East Germany's Bernd and Jörg Landvoigt became the first identical twins to win Olympic gold when successful in what sport at the 1976 Montreal Games?
3. Miklos Nemeth of Hungary claimed the Olympic javelin title in 1976, but in which other athletics event had his father Imre taken gold in 1948?
4. Name the American brother and sister who both won athletics medals at the 1984 Los Angeles Olympics.
5. What was the surname of the British brothers who triumphed in the coxed pairs rowing event in 1992, one of whom came out of retirement to win bronze in 2012 at the age of 40?
6. At Barcelona 1992, in what sport did two pairs of identical twin sisters win gold and silver medals in the same event?
7. Emanoul Aghassian, the father of Andre Agassi, the 1996 men's singles tennis champion, boxed for which Middle Eastern nation at two Olympics?
8. The great nephew of which famous American writer gained an athletics medal at the 2004 Olympics?
9. At the 2008 Games, the Hochschorner twins, Peter and Pavol, became the first slalom canoeists to earn three Olympic gold medals. What East European nation are they from?
10. What was the surname of the pair of brothers from Coleraine, Northern Ireland, who helped Great Britain win silver in the lightweight fours rowing event at London 2012?

Answers on page 240

Find the Lady

1. The winner of three swimming medals at the 1924 Olympics, who made history two years later as the first woman to swim the English Channel?
2. Name the Czech athlete who won discus gold in 1956 and, after a 'Cold War romance' that began in the Olympic Village, married the American hammer champion Hal Connolly?
3. Which future queen consort represented Greece in two sailing events at the 1960 Rome Olympics?
4. Name the American swimmer, a descendant of Prussian and Swedish nobility, who won three Olympic golds in 1960.
5. In gymnastics, which Soviet star claimed the women's individual all-around title at the 1972 Games in Munich?
6. In 1984, which American athlete was the winner of the inaugural Olympic marathon for women.
7. Which female US sprinter retained her Olympic 100m title by one-thousandth of a second in 1996?
8. Name the British competitor who made history in 2000 as the first female Olympic champion in modern pentathlon.
9. Which British swimmer placed third behind team-mate Rebecca Adlington in the women's 400m freestyle final at Beijing 2008?
10. At London 2012, which female Ethiopian distance runner won gold at 5000m to reclaim the title she had first won in 2004?

Answers on page 240

Great Britain at the Summer Olympics

Part 1 (1896–1976)

1. Launceston Elliot became Great Britain's first Olympic champion when he won gold in which sport at the 1896 Games?
2. Which British woman made history as the first individual female Olympic champion when she claimed the women's singles title in tennis in 1900?
3. County champions Cornwall won a silver medal representing Great Britain in what sport at the 1908 London Games?
4. The only British Olympic champions in two different sports, Rob Derbyshire and Paul Radmilovic won golds in the early 20th century in swimming and what other sport?
5. Blackpool-born Lucy Morton made history in 1924 when she became the first British woman to claim an individual Olympic title in what sport?
6. Nicknamed the 'Peerless Peer', who won an athletics gold medal in 1928 and was chairman of the organizing committee for the London Games of 1948?
7. The winner of two silver medals, Somerset fruit farmer Bill Hoskyns competed in which sport at six Olympics between 1956 and 1976?
8. Britain's youngest ever Summer Olympian, Ken Lester was only 13 when he competed in what sport at the 1960 Games?
9. Twice a bronze medallist, which British male show jumper competed in his first Olympics in 1960 and his last in 1988?
10. Apart from the 400m, at which she won a silver medal, which two other athletics events did Lillian Board compete in at the 1968 Mexico Olympics?

Answers on page 241

117

Great Britain at the Summer Olympics

Part 2 (1976–2008)

1. Who won Britain's only athletics medal of the 1976 Games?
2. In which athletics track event did Shirley Strong, a 20-a-day smoker, win a silver medal at the 1984 Olympics?
3. Who partnered Steve Redgrave to victory in the coxless pairs rowing event at Seoul 1988?
4. In what sport did Britain's Simon Terry earn two bronze medals at the 1992 Games in Barcelona?
5. In which athletics event at Sydney 2000 did Darren Campbell earn a silver medal for Britain?
6. Which female British equestrian gained her third Olympic medal in 2004?
7. In which sport did British pair Nick Rogers and Joe Glanfield win silver medals in both 2004 and 2008?
8. Name the 38-year-old swimmer who carried the British flag at the opening ceremony of the Beijing Olympics.
9. Which female cyclist won Great Britain's first gold medal of the 2008 Games?
10. In gymnastics in 2008, who finished third in the men's pommel horse final to give Britain its first Olympic medal in an individual gymnastics event for 100 years?

Answers on page 241

Great Britain at the Summer Olympics

Part 3 – London 2012

1. Which female rowing duo not only provided Great Britain with its first gold medal of the 2012 Games but also made history as the first British women to claim an Olympic title in this sport?
2. Name the two British women who each won two gold medals at London 2012.
3. Which British swimmer set three national records on his way to winning a silver medal and was only denied gold by a world record performance from a Hungarian rival?
4. Before taking individual bronze in the 10m platform diving event, Tom Daley had placed fourth in the synchronised competition when partnering which other British diver?
5. In which sport at London 2012 were the Great Britain teams captained by Barry Middleton and Kate Walsh?
6. Name the rower from Northern Ireland who won a gutsy bronze in the men's single sculls event.
7. In which event did Jessica Ennis set a world best time on her way to winning the heptathlon title?
8. In what sport did Team GB achieve its only 1-2 finish at London 2012, Tim Baillie and Etienne Stott winning gold and team-mates David Florence and Richard Hounslow silver?
9. The oldest member of Team GB at London 2012, Richard Davison, took part in which sport aged 56 ?
10. Name the Bath University student who won Team GB's 65th and last medal of the Games when runner-up in the final event, the women's modern pentathlon.

Answers on page 242

Memorable Moments

1. Which British runner won 800m gold in world record time at the 1964 Tokyo Olympics?
2. In 1976, Japan's Shun Fujimoto performed with a broken kneecap to ensure his nation won an event in what sport?
3. Why did Canadian sailor Lawrence Lemieux receive an award after dropping from second place to finish 22nd in his event at Seoul 1988?
4. At Barcelona 1992, which British competitor tore a hamstring during an athletics race and was helped to finish by his father, who entered the track without credentials?
5. Name the famous sportsman who lit the cauldron in a moving climax to the opening ceremony of the 1996 Games.
6. Eric 'The Eel' Moussambani, the novice swimmer whose tenacity and bravery made headlines at Sydney 2000, represented which central African country?
7. Which event at Athens 2004 saw the leader attacked by a defrocked Irish priest and dragged into the crowd?
8. In the women's 10 metre air pistol shooting event in 2008, medallists from which two warring countries shared a kiss on the podium and asked for an end to hostilities?
9. Earning the nickname 'Issaka the Otter', Niger's Hamadou Djibo Issaka received a standing ovation from the 25,000-strong crowd after finishing a distant last when competing in what sport at London 2012?
10. Manteo Mitchell (USA) ran approximately 200 metres with a broken leg when competing in which athletics event in London?

Answers on page 242

Multi-talented Summer Olympians

Part 1 – Other sports

1. In 1896, Australia's Edwin Flack completed an 800-1500m double in athletics and then, partnered by a British discus thrower, took a bronze medal in what sport?
2. The only Olympic medallist in three different sports at a single Games, Frank Kugler (USA) won medals in 1904 in wrestling, tug of war, and which other power sport?
3. Johnny Douglas, an Olympic boxing champion at the 1908 Games, later captained the England team in what sport?
4. Described as 'Britain's greatest sportsman', who won Olympic medals in tennis in 1920, played football for England, was a scratch golfer, and once defeated Charlie Chaplin at table tennis using a butter knife instead of a bat?
5. Who claimed two Olympic titles in women's athletics in 1932, and later became the world's dominant player in women's golf?
6. Which US sprinter gained two Olympic gold medals in the 1960s and played in a winning Super Bowl team in the 1970s.
7. Roswitha Krause earned two handball medals for East Germany in the period 1976–80, but in which sport had she been an Olympic medallist in 1968?
8. Clara Hughes (USA) took three medals in speed skating at the Winter Olympics in 2002–06, having earlier won two bronzes in what sport at the 1996 Summer Games in Atlanta?
9. The only female British Olympic medallist in two sports, who took a silver in rowing in 2004 and a gold in cycling in 2008?
10. After previously competing in swimming and triathlon, Sheila Taormina (USA) became the first female Olympian to compete in three sports when she took part in what sport at Beijing 2008?

Answers on page 243

Multi-talented Summer Olympians

Part 2 – Other fields

1. Which future World War II American general finished fifth in the modern pentathlon at the 1912 Olympics in Stockholm?
2. Before finding fame as a world authority in the field of baby and child care, Dr Benjamin Spock won Olympic gold at the 1924 Paris Games as a member of a US team in what sport?
3. Arthur Porrit, who earned 100m bronze in athletics in 1924, later served as King's Surgeon to George VI and as Governor General of which Commonwealth country?
4. Who claimed an Olympic swimming title in 1932 and later played Flash Gordon, Tarzan and Buck Rogers in films?
5. Name the famous British naturalist who won a bronze medal in sailing at the 1936 Berlin Games.
6. Harold Sakata, a silver medallist in weightlifting in 1948, later played a memorable villain in which James Bond film?
7. Name the French concert pianist who claimed two athletics titles at the 1948 London Games.
8. James Wolfensohn, a member of Australia's fencing team at the 1956 Olympics, later served as president of which international economic organisation?
9. Which future politician ran for Great Britain at the 1964 Games in Tokyo, reaching the semi-finals of the 200m?
10. Which Olympic champion of the 1960s won the first *World Superstars* competition in 1977 and had a role in the TV sitcom *Soap*?

Answers on page 243

Summer Olympics Legends

Part 1 (1920–1976)

1. How many gold medals did Finnish distance runner Paavo Nurmi win in his sparkling Olympic career?
2. Much to Adolf Hitler's displeasure, black athlete Jesse Owens (USA) was the star of the 1936 Berlin Games after claiming four titles: in the 100m, 200m, 4x100m, and which other event?
3. In 1948, 'Flying Dutchwoman' Fanny Blankers-Koen won gold in the 100m, 200m, 4x100m and which other athletics event?
4. How many Olympic titles did Czech distance runner Emil Zatopek gain in his outstanding career?
5. Name the Soviet gymnast who amassed a female record of 18 Olympic medals between 1956 and 1964.
6. In 1960, who ran barefoot through the streets of Rome to become the first black African to win an Olympic marathon and then retained his title four years later in Tokyo?
7. Who claimed his fourth consecutive Olympic crown in the same athletics event at the 1968 Mexico Games?
8. Which tiny Soviet gymnast was nicknamed the 'Munchkin of Munich' after winning three golds in 1972?
9. How many gold medals did US swimmer Mark Spitz win in his Olympic career?
10. Name the distance runner who completed a 5000-10000m double at both the Munich and Montreal Olympics.

Answers on page 244

Summer Olympics Legends

Part 2 (1980–2012)

1. Nikolai Andrianov of the Soviet Union ended his prolific Olympic career in 1980 after amassing 15 medals (a male record at the time) in what sport?
2. How many Olympic medals did Sebastian Coe win?
3. In which event in 1996 did Carl Lewis claim his ninth and last Olympic title?
4. The sailor Hubert Raudaschl, who appeared at a then-record ninth Olympics in 1996, competed for what European nation?
5. Which American runner won his fourth Olympic gold when retaining his 400m crown at the 2000 Games in Sydney?
6. Name the male Australian swimmer who won nine Olympic medals, including five golds, between 2000 and 2004 and worked as a pundit for BBC Television at London 2012.
7. At London 2012, US swimmer Michael Phelps became the most decorated Olympian of all time after taking his medal tally to how many?
8. Sir Chris Hoy made history as the first Briton to win six Olympic gold medals with victory in which cycling event at London 2012?
9. Who became the most successful sailor in Olympic history after winning his fourth consecutive gold at London 2012?
10. What was the Olympic record time set by Usain Bolt when he retained his 100m title in 2012?

Answers on page 244

The Summer Olympics at the Movies

1. Which German film director made *Olympia* (1938), a ground-breaking documentary of the 1936 Games in Berlin?
2. Played by Warner Oland, which fictional detective battled enemy agents at the Olympics in a 1937 film that included footage from the Berlin Games?
3. Which famous Hollywood actor starred in the 1951 autobiographical film *Jim Thorpe – All-American*, which told the story of the double Olympic champion and featured archive footage from two Games?
4. Which major figure in Japanese cinema directed and co-wrote the 1965 documentary film *Tokyo Olympiad*?
5. Better known nowadays as a food critic, which British film producer and director directed *The Games*, a 1970 drama film about four competitors in an Olympic marathon?
6. Which British actor and screenwriter won the Academy Award for Best Original Screenplay for his script for *Chariots of Fire*?
7. The Oscar-winning documentary *One Day in September* (released in 1992) chronicles the dramatic events at which Summer Olympics?
8. Japanese equestrian Takeichi Nishi, the winner of Olympic gold in 1932, later served in World War II and was depicted as a main character in which 2006 film directed by Clint Eastwood?
9. What 2008 Australian film recounts the highly controversial 'Black Power' protest at the 1968 Mexico Olympics?
10. Which 2012 film tells the story of a fictional British female sprint relay team in their quest to win Olympic gold?

Answers on page 245

The Summer Olympics and Music

1. Name the famous German composer who wrote an Olympic Hymn for the 1936 Berlin Games and conducted the Berlin Philharmonic Orchestra when they performed it at the opening ceremony.
2. Which composer won a Grammy award for composing the theme for Los Angeles 1984, *Olympic Fanfare and Theme*?
3. Which Whitney Houston song was used by the American broadcaster NBC for its coverage of the 1988 Seoul Olympics?
4. The two main songs for the 1992 Summer Olympics were *Barcelona* and *Amigos Para Siempre* (*Friends for Life*). The latter song was performed at the closing ceremony by Sarah Brightman and which famous tenor?
5. Which female singer performed *Georgia on My Mind*, Georgia's official state song, at the opening ceremony of the 1996 Atlanta Games?
6. Featuring contributions from the likes of Sting, Lenny Kravitz and Destiny's Child, what was the title of the official pop album of the 2004 Athens Olympics?
7. Which British female singer performed at the 2008 closing ceremony as part of the handover of the Games from Beijing to London?
8. In July 2012, which band represented Wales at the Opening Ceremony Celebration Concert held in London's Hyde Park?
9. Which Scottish female singer performed at both the opening and closing ceremonies of London 2012?
10. Who performed his new single at the closing ceremony of London 2012, leading to criticism that he had used the event to 'plug' his new material?

Answers on page 245

The One and Only

Part 1 – General

1. Including the 1906 Intercalated Games, who is the only person to have won 10 Olympic gold medals in athletics?
2. Gillian Sheen is Great Britain's only Olympic champion in what sport?
3. Billy Mills is the only US Olympic champion in which athletics track event?
4. In which field event in athletics is Cyrus Young the United States' only Olympic champion?
5. Who is the only Briton to win Olympic medals both before and after World War Two?
6. In tennis, who is the only Swiss player to have claimed a singles title at the Olympics?
7. What nationality was fencer Aladir Gerevich, the only man to win six consecutive Olympic titles?
8. Who is the only Briton to win an athletics medal at three Olympics?
9. Germany's Birgitte Fischer, the only woman to earn gold medals at six consecutive Games, achieved this feat in which sport?
10. What is the only nation to have won at least one gold medal at every Summer Games?

Answers on page 246

The One and Only

Part 2 (1908–2012)

1. The Olympics visited Scotland for the only time in 1908, when a rowing event was held on which river?
2. British athlete Philip Noel-Baker, a silver medallist at 1500m in 1920, is the only Olympian to have won which international award?
3. Britain's Philip Neame, a shooting champion at the 1924 Games, is the only person to win an Olympic gold medal and which military honour?
4. The only winner of a gold medal at both Summer and Winter Games, Eddie Eagan (USA) took bobsleigh team gold in 1932 after claiming an individual title in what sport in 1920?
5. Felipe Muñoz's victory in the 200m breaststroke at the 1968 Olympics remains the only swimming title for which nation?
6. Christa Luding-Rothenburger (GDR) is the only competitor to win medals at the Winter and Summer Olympics in the same year. After winning speed skating gold in Calgary in 1988, she added a silver medal in what sport in Seoul?
7. The only person to have won medals at both the Olympic and Paralympic Games, Hungary's Pál Szekeres was successful in which sport in the 1980s/90s?
8. Gouda Shouaa, who won the 1996 heptathlon title, is the only Olympic champion from which Middle Eastern country?
9. Who was the only British track cyclist to return home from the Beijing Olympics without a medal?
10. Oussami Mellouli's victory in the men's 10km marathon swimming event gave which North African country its only gold medal at London 2012?

Answers on page 246

Quote...Unquote

1. Which Olympic champion said, "Hitler didn't snub me – it was FDR who snubbed me. The president didn't even send me a telegram."?
2. After winning an athletics title in 1948, which American teenager said his next goal was to start shaving?
3. Commentating on David Hemery's runaway victory in the 400m hurdles final at the 1968 Mexico Olympics, David Coleman said, "And who cares who's third?". Which British athlete was in fact third?
4. After winning Olympic gold in boxing in 1972, who refused offers to turn professional by saying: "I wouldn't exchange my piece of Cuba for all the money they could give me."?
5. Which athlete tempted fate by saying of his Olympic prospects for 1980, "I have a 90% chance of winning the 1500 metres."?
6. When commentating on the men's hockey final in 1988, who said after a goal for Great Britain: "Where were the Germans? But frankly, who cares?"
7. At the 1996 Atlanta Olympics, of which world record-breaker did David Coleman say, "Surely this man is not human?"?
8. Name the American swimmer who dismissed Australia's chances of winning the men's 4x100m freestyle final at Sydney 2000 by saying, "We will smash them like guitars" – words that came back to haunt him after the home nation won gold.
9. After watching his son win gold in swimming at London 2012, who said: "It's unbelievable. Unbelievable. Unbelievable. Look at him, he's a beautiful boy. Look at him, he's crying like me."
10. On his way to retaining a title at London 2012, which Briton said of his rivals: "They teamed up on me. Big mistake, because I'm angry. And you don't want to make me angry."

Answers on page 247

The USA at the Summer Olympics

Part 1 (1900–1952)

1. In 1900, Margaret Abbott became the first female US Olympic champion when she triumphed in what outdoor sport?
2. Nicknamed the 'Milwaukee Meteor', which US sprinter gained three gold medals at the 1904 Olympics?
3. In which team sport are the USA the reigning Olympic champions, having beaten France in the last final in 1924?
4. Husband and wife Charles and Betty Pinkston won seven Olympic medals in what sport in the 1920s?
5. Which future World War II military leader headed the American team at the 1928 Amsterdam Games as president of the US Olympic Committee?
6. Name the American athlete who won gold in the women's high jump in 1932 after the western-roll style used by compatriot Mildred ('Babe') Didriksen was ruled illegal after both women had cleared the same world record height in the jump-off.
7. Favoured to win gold at the 1936 Berlin Olympics, which female American swimmer was banned from competing by the US team after misbehaving on the boat to Europe?
8. In 1948, Audrey ('Mickey') Patterson became the first African-American woman to win an Olympic medal when taking bronze in what athletics event?
9. At the age of 59, Everard Endt claimed a title in what sport at the 1952 Helsinki Games?
10. The winner of the 3000m steeplechase in 1952, Horace Ashenfelter, worked for which agency of the US government?

Answers on page 247

The USA at the Summer Olympics

Part 2 (1960–2012)

1. Which American long jumper gained three Olympic medals in the 1960s?
2. Bill Bradley, who later served 18 years in the US Senate, won gold in what team sport at the 1964 Tokyo Games?
3. Name the charismatic American distance runner who narrowly failed to win a medal at the 1972 Munich Olympics.
4. Which American swimmer was one of the stars of the 1976 Montreal Games after collecting four gold medals and one silver?
5. The oldest champion at the 1984 Los Angeles Games, Seattle-born William Earl Buchan claimed a title in what sport at the age of 49?
6. Name the female American swimmer who won three individual gold medals at the 1988 Seoul Olympics.
7. Who was the last President of the United States to officially open a Summer Olympic Games?
8. At Sydney 2000, in what team sport did the USA triumph after losing three successive matches early in the tournament?
9. Which US sprinter raced to victory in the men's 100m final at the 2004 Olympics, then served a four-year ban for a doping offence, only to return to win two medals at London 2012?
10. Kim Rhode became the first American to win medals in individual events at five consecutive Olympics after securing gold in what sport at London 2012?

Answers on page 248

Trivia Teasers

Part 1 (1904–1956)

1. What physical handicap did George Eyser (USA) overcome to win six medals in gymnastics at the 1904 Games in St Louis?
2. In 1908, Ireland beat Germany 3–1 in the final of what very unusual demonstration sport?
3. What North African city was unsuccessful in the bid election for the 1916 Games (later cancelled of course owing to WWI)?
4. Hawaiian-born Duke Kahanamoku, an Olympic champion swimmer in the 1920s, was a pioneer of what other aquatic sport?
5. The future King of which European nation won a gold medal in sailing at the 1928 Amsterdam Games?
6. At the 1932 Los Angeles Olympics, in what athletics event was a world record credited to the runner-up rather than the winner?
7. In 1936, who fondled a female athletics champion and invited her to his mountain retreat?
8. The US flag bearer at the opening ceremony of the 1948 London Games, Ralph Craig, had taken two Olympic titles all of 36 years earlier in which sport?
9. Britain's Ken Richmond, who found fame as the bare-chested man who banged the gong in the opening credits for Rank films, won a bronze medal in what sport in 1952?
10. Which female Australian swimmer belied her surname to win two Olympic gold medals in the 1950s?

Answers on page 248

Trivia Teasers

Part 2 (1960–2008)

1. In 1960, which distinguished spectator watched the Olympic rowing events on Lake Albano from his summer residence?
2. Which British Olympic champion of the 1960s was named by Mick Jagger as his 'dream date' and approached by film producers wanting her to play a 'woman James Bond'?
3. Which world-record breaking athletics champion from the 1968 Mexico Games shares his name with a modern-day British stand-up comedian and actor?
4. Which star of British athletics broke down in tears after failing to gain an Olympic medal in 1976?
5. Which British Olympic fencer (who was knighted in 1993) became the only the third female member of the International Olympic Committee upon her appointment in 1982?
6. What European nation boycotted its fourth consecutive Summer Olympics in 1988?
7. The route of the 1996 Olympic marathon took runners past several sites associated with which iconic historical figure?
8. A fictional account of a South Korean women's team at Athens 2004, *Forever the Moment* (2008) is believed to be the first film based on which sport?
9. Benjamin Boukpeti earned a bronze medal in canoeing in 2008 to give which west African nation its first ever Olympic medal?
10. A Cubist-style sheepdog named *Cobi* was the official mascot of which Games of this period?

Answers on page 249

Trivia Teasers

Part 3 (London 2012/general)

1. In the BBC TV spoof documentary series *Twenty Twelve*, which satirised preparations for the London Games, who played Ian Fletcher, Head of Deliverance of the Olympic Deliverance Commission?
2. In which sport did Poland's Bartłomiej Bonk win a bronze medal at London 2012?
3. New Zealand's Logan Campbell competed in taekwondo in 2012 after funding himself through the proceeds of what unusual business venture for an Olympic hopeful?
4. Which sport did Malaysia's Nur Suryani Mohamed Taibi compete in at London 2012 while eight months pregnant?
5. Team GB's Lawrence Clarke, who placed fourth in the 110m hurdles final in 2012, is a distant relative of which 20th century US President?
6. Which Caribbean sprinter was sent home from London 2012 for visiting his wife and children at a hotel outside the Olympic Village?
7. In what sport at London 2012 did Colombia's Lady Andrade receive a two-match ban for punching an opponent?
8. What is most populous nation never to have won a medal at the Summer Olympics?
9. Which North American city has never hosted the Summer Games, having failed a record seven times to win a bid election?
10. Of the nations never to have staged an Olympics, which one has won the most medals in the history of the Summer Games?

Answers on page 249

Last but not Least

Part 1 – General
1. Which sport last featured at the 1904 Olympics but will reappear at the 2016 Games?
2. Name the last Welshman to win an individual gold medal at the Summer Olympics.
3. Who were the last team to beat the USA in women's Olympic basketball?
4. In boxing, who was the last American to win the Olympic super heavyweight title?
5. What was the last European nation to be crowned Olympic champions in men's football?
6. Which track event in men's athletics was held for the last time at the 1952 Olympics?
7. Which Asian country won its last men's Olympic hockey title in 1984?
8. Who was the last American tennis player to win the men's singles at the Olympics?
9. What was the last nation apart from China to win an Olympic title in table tennis?
10. Laura Asadauskaite's victory in the women's modern pentathlon ensured that the last gold at London 2012 went to which European country?

Answers on page 250

Last but not Least

Part 2 – Great Britain

1. Who was the last Briton to set a world record when winning an Olympic title in athletics?
2. In which year did Great Britain last win gold in Olympic hockey?
3. Who was the last British man to claim an Olympic title in swimming?
4. In which team sport did Britain win its fourth and last Olympic gold medal in 1920?
5. Leslie Law is the last British man to win an individual Olympic title in which sport?
6. Prior to 2012, in which year had Great Britain last competed at an Olympic football tournament?
7. Who was the last British man to win the Olympic 400 metres in athletics?
8. In what year did Great Britain last fail to win an Olympic title in rowing?
9. Prior to Chris Hoy in 2008, who had been the last Briton to win three gold medals at a single Olympics?
10. Name the boxer who won Great Britain's 29th and last gold of London 2012.

Answers on page 250

PART B –

WINTER OLYMPICS QUESTIONS

5. WINTER OLYMPIC HISTORY

Overview

1. Which French ski resort staged the inaugural Winter Olympics in 1924?
2. Great Britain claimed its first Winter Olympic title when taking gold in what sport at the 1924 Games?
3. Which historical figure officially opened the 1936 Winter Olympics in Garmisch-Partenkirchen?
4. In 1948, which venue staged the Winter Games for the second time?
5. Name the first Asian city to host the Winter Olympics.
6. Which European city staged both the 1964 and 1976 Winter Games?
7. In 1984, in which city did Britain's Jayne Torvill and Christopher Dean strike Olympic gold in figure skating?
8. Name the captain of the Great Britain team that claimed the women's curling title at Salk Lake City in 2002.
9. Who won gold for Britain in the skeleton at the 2010 Vancouver Games?
10. Which Russian city will host the 2014 Winter Olympics?

Answers on page 251

Chamonix 1924

1. These Games were originally called the *Semaine Internationale des Sports d'Hiver.* What is the English translation of this phrase?
2. Charles Jewtraw (USA) became the first Winter Olympic champion with victory in which sport in 1924?
3. Name either of the sports here that had previously featured at the 1920 Summer Olympics in Antwerp.
4. The winner of three gold medals in Chamonix, what nationality was speed skater Clas Thunberg?
5. Norway's Thorleif Haug won three titles in which sport?
6. Which European country won the first men's bobsleigh title?
7. An early version of biathlon, what sport was a medal event for the first and last time at these Olympics?
8. Which nation dominated the ice hockey competition, winning all its six matches and conceding only three goals?
9. In what sport did Britain's Ethel Muckelt win a bronze medal?
10. Which country topped the medal table at these Games?

Answers on page 251

St Moritz 1928

1. The continent of Asia made its debut at the Winter Olympics with the appearance of which nation?
2. Which Central American nation made its debut at these Games?
3. The skeleton sled was introduced here and staged on what famous toboggan track?
4. For the only time in Winter Olympic history, how many competitors were allowed in a bobsleigh team?
5. Unseasonably warm weather caused the cancellation of an event in what sport?
6. A future great of the sport, which Norwegian skater gained the first of her three Olympic figure skating titles at the age of 15?
7. Gillis Grafström, who won a third consecutive gold in men's figure skating, represented which nation?
8. Name either of the two sports in which Norway's Johan Grøttumsbråten won gold in St Moritz.
9. Great Britain's only medal at these Games came when John, Earl of Northesk claimed a bronze in what sport?
10. Which nation finished runner-up to Norway in the medal table?

Answers on page 252

Lake Placid 1932

1. Which future President of the United States officially opened these Games?
2. Mollie Phillips became the first female flag bearer in Olympic history when she carried which country's flag in the opening ceremony?
3. Name the sport that was a demonstration sport for women in Lake Placid.
4. After claiming a boxing title at the 1920 Summer Games in Antwerp, Eddie Eagan (USA) achieved a still-unique double by winning Olympic gold in what winter sport in 1932?
5. Which European nation took a bronze medal in the ice hockey competition?
6. Name either of the long-distance speed skating events at which Irving Jaffee (USA) was crowned Olympic champion.
7. Figure skater Karl Schäfer won gold for what European nation in the men's singles event?
8. The cross-country skiing events were held over 18km and which other, longer distance?
9. Which Scandinavian country completed a clean sweep of the medals in the only ski jumping event?
10. What demonstration sport featuring animals featured in the schedule for the only time in Winter Olympic history?

Answers on page 252

Garmisch-Partenkirchen 1936

1. A main feature of later Games, what sport made its first appearance at these Winter Olympics?
2. Which East European nation made its Winter Olympic debut in Garmisch-Partenkirchen?
3. The most successful competitor here was Norway's Ivar Ballangrud, with three gold medals and a silver in which sport?
4. Which central European nation took its only gold at these Games with victory in the four-man bobsleigh event?
5. In what sport did Great Britain win a surprise gold medal, thereby claiming its only Winter Olympic title of the 1930s?
6. British teenager Cecilia Colledge won a silver medal in which sport?
7. A relay over what distance in total was added to the cross-country skiing programme?
8. Norway's Birger Rudd retained his Winter Olympic title in what sport?
9. Both combined events in Alpine skiing (men's, women's) were won by competitors from which country?
10. Which nation headed the medal table with seven golds?

Answers on page 253

St Moritz 1948

1. Which two nations were, unsurprisingly, not invited to take part in these Olympics?
2. What South American country made its Winter Olympic debut at these Games?
3. There were two demonstration sports here, military patrol and which other?
4. Which East European nation was runner-up to Canada in the ice hockey competition?
5. On his way to claiming the men's singles title in figure skating, Dick Button (USA) became the first person to complete what jump in competition?
6. Name the French skier who won as a medal in all three Alpine events: gold in the downhill and combined, and bronze in the slalom.
7. What nation dominated the women's Alpine events, winning five out of a possible nine medals?
8. Which central European country saw its two teams place first and second in the two-man bobsleigh event?
9. Which future legend of winter sports took gold in the skeleton event to give Italy its first ever Winter Olympic title?
10. Name either of the European nations that finished joint-top of the medal table after each winning 4 golds and 10 medals in total.

Answers on page 253

Oslo 1952

1. The opening day of these Games coincided with the funeral of which monarch, prompting Commonwealth competitors to wear black armbands in tribute?
2. Which Antipodean nation made its Winter Olympic debut in Oslo?
3. Star of the Games was Norway's Hjalmar Andersen, who took three gold medals in what sport?
4. Who became Great Britain's first female Winter Olympic champion when she claimed the ladies' singles title in figure skating?
5. In which sport did a 19-year-old American woman, Andrea Mead Lawrence, earn two gold medals?
6. Lydia Wideman of Finland became the first female Olympic champion in what sport?
7. Which country won its sixth successive Olympic ski jumping title in 1952?
8. In figure skating, the mixed pairs competition was won by a husband and wife team from what European country?
9. Similar to ice hockey, what sport of Scandinavian origin was the only demonstration sport in Oslo?
10. Martin Stokken, who helped Norway take a relay silver in cross country skiing, had placed fourth in what long distance athletics event at the 1948 Summer Games in London?

Answers on page 254

Cortina D'Ampezzo 1956

1. Cortina had originally been scheduled to host the Winter Olympics in which year?
2. These were the last Games at which events in what sport were held outdoors?
3. Which nation marked its Winter Olympic debut by winning the most medals?
4. The undoubted star in Cortina, which Austrian skier became the first Olympic champion in all three Alpine events?
5. Norwegian dominance of Olympic ski jumping ended when jumpers from which country took the first two places in the competition?
6. Achieving two gold medals and two world records, Yevgeny Grishin (USSR) was the stand-out performer in what sport?
7. Alpine skier Chiharu Igaya won the first Winter Olympic medal for Japan when runner-up in which event?
8. What Nordic country gained six medals in cross-country skiing?
9. In the pairs event in figure skating, two siblings from which East European nation retained their bronze medal from 1952?
10. Which country brushed aside the USA to win the ice hockey final by an impressive 4–0 scoreline?

Answers on page 254

Squaw Valley 1960

1. Name the Vice President of the United Sates who officially opened the Games.
2. Which sport was added to the schedule for these Winter Olympics?
3. What sport was dropped from the programme for financial reasons, meaning it was absent for the only time in Olympic history?
4. In which sport were women allowed to compete for the first time at a Winter Olympics?
5. The winner of the only event in ski jumping, the men's normal hill, came from what European nation?
6. In figure skating, triple world champions Bob Paul and Barbara Wagner won gold for which country in the pairs event?
7. In what sport was Penny Pitou (USA) the only competitor to gain two medals?
8. Finland's Veikko Hakulinen took a full set of medals (gold, silver, bronze) in which sport?
9. What country pulled off a major surprise to by taking its first Olympic title in ice hockey?
10. In what sport did future husband and wife David Jenkins and Carol Heiss (both USA) win gold medals?

Answers on page 255

Innsbruck 1964

1. Name either of the Asian nations that made their Winter Olympic debut in Innsbruck.
2. What innovation at these Games aided judging of events and provided electronic timing?
3. Which sport was contested here for the first time at a Winter Games?
4. Star performer was the Soviet Union's Lydia Skoblikova, who won four golds in what sport?
5. The first sisters to win gold at the same Winter Games, Alpine skiers Christine and Marielle Goitschel represented which nation?
6. The Netherlands claimed its first ever Winter Olympic title when Sjoukje Dijkstra triumphed in what sport?
7. Which country provided the first two finishers in the biathlon?
8. In the four-man bobsleigh, hot favourites Austria could only take silver as what country took a shock gold?
9. Name the duo whose victory in the two-man bobsleigh gave Great Britain its first Winter Olympic title since 1952.
10. Which European nation was runner-up to the Soviet Union in the medal table?

Answers on page 255

Grenoble 1968

1. Which famous political leader officially opened these Games?
2. Olympic history was made as the IOC ordered testing of competitors in what two areas?
3. Name the North African nation that made its Winter Olympic debut here.
4. Which Frenchman became the star of the Games after winning all three titles in Alpine skiing?
5. The oldest medallist in Grenoble at the age of 40, Italy's Eugenio Monti won two golds in what sport?
6. Successful in the ladies singles event in figure skating, Peggy Fleming was which country's only champion at these Games?
7. Swedish woman Toini Gustafsson dominated what sport by taking two individual golds and a relay silver?
8. A married couple from which nation successfully defended their pairs figure skating title from Innsbruck?
9. What East European country won its first, and so far only, medal at the Winter Games with a bronze in bobsleigh?
10. In an event in which sport were three American women each awarded a silver medal after a triple dead-heat for second place?

Answers on page 256

Sapporo 1972

1. Name the Japanese emperor who officially opened these Games.
2. Which populous Asian country made its Winter Olympic debut here?
3. What nation refused to send an ice hockey team, arguing that professional ice hockey players from Communist nations were permitted to compete with no restrictions?
4. One of the star performers in Sapporo was Ard Schenk of the Netherlands, who won three titles in which sport?
5. In what sport did Galina Kulakova (USSR) win all three women's titles?
6. Norway's Magnar Solberg retained his Olympic title in which sport?
7. In ski jumping, what nation achieved a clean sweep of the medals in the men's 70m event?
8. What nationality was Marie-Thérès Nadig, surprise winner of both the downhill and the giant slalom events?
9. Which European country gained its only title in Winter Olympic history when taking gold in the men's slalom title in Alpine skiing?
10. What European nation was runner-up to the Soviet Union in the medal table?

Answers on page 256

Innsbruck 1976

1. Innsbruck was chosen as host city after the winner of the bid election withdrew. Which North American city had originally been awarded the Games?
2. Name either of the European microstates that made their Winter Olympic debuts in 1976.
3. As in 1964, events in what sport were held outdoors in the *Olympia Eisschnellaufbahn*?
4. Star performer here was Alpine skier Rosi Mittermaier, who won two golds and a silver representing which country?
5. In Alpine skiing, who achieved the highest average speed then recorded in an Olympic downhill race when winning the men's downhill title?
6. Which country won its fourth consecutive title in ice hockey?
7. Who struck gold in figure skating to give Great Britain its first Winter Olympic title in 12 years?
8. Which American woman won figure skating gold – and set a new fashion trend with her 'wedge' hairstyle?
9. All five luge and bobsleigh titles were claimed by competitors from which Soviet bloc country?
10. In what sport did Finland's Heikki Ikola earn two silver medals?

Answers on page 257

Lake Placid 1980

1. What large Asian country made its Winter Olympic debut here?
2. Name the Vice President of the United States who opened the Games.
3. Which American speed skater became the first person to win five individual gold medals at a single Winter Games?
4. In figure skating, whose victory gave Great Britain its second consecutive title in the men's singles event?
5. In Alpine skiing, Hanni Wenzel won the women's giant slalom and slalom for what tiny European nation?
6. In the men's events in Alpine skiing, which Swedish star triumphed in both the giant slalom and the slalom?
7. East Germany's Ulrich Wehling claim his third consecutive Olympic title in what sport?
8. What nickname was given to the United States' shock defeat of the USSR in the final round of the ice hockey competition?
9. In which sport did Nikolay Zimyatov (USSR) earn three gold medals?
10. What nation gained the most medals overall but finished second in the medal table by virtue of winning fewer golds (9) than the Soviet Union (10)?

Answers on page 257

Sarajevo 1984

1. These were the first Games to be held during the term of office of which president of the IOC?
2. Which North African country made its Winter Olympic debut in Sarajevo?
3. What now-defunct European nation won its first Winter Olympic medal when Jure Franko gained a silver in the giant slalom event in Alpine skiing?
4. The most successful competitor was Finland's Marja-Liisa Hämäläinen, who took three golds in which sport?
5. Debi Thomas (USA) became the first black competitor to win a medal in what sport?
6. In which sport did Norway's Eirik Kvalfoss gain a full set of medals (gold, silver, bronze)?
7. In men's Alpine skiing, who became the first American to win an Olympic downhill event?
8. Which country won nine of the twelve medals in women's speed skating?
9. Gaétan Boucher won two golds in men's speed skating for what country?
10. Traditionally strong in winter sports, which central European nation gained just one medal (a bronze) at these Games?

Answers on page 258

Calgary 1988

1. The Governor General of Canada, Jeanne Suavé, officially opened the Games on behalf of whom?
2. In Alpine skiing, which event for both men and women was added to the Olympic schedule?
3. Events in what sport were held in an indoor rink for the first time at a Winter Olympics?
4. Also for the first time, events in which sport were held on artificial snow?
5. Which sport did Finland's Matti Nykänen dominate by winning three gold medals?
6. The leading female performer was Yvonne van Gennip of the Netherlands, who claimed three titles in what sport?
7. In figure skating, which popular East German retained her ladies' singles title from Sarajevo?
8. Nicknamed 'La Bomba', which Italian star won two golds in men's Alpine skiing?
9. Frank-Peter Roetsch of East Germany became the first winner of both individual events in what sport?
10. Which now-defunct nation topped the medal table for the final time?

Answers on page 258

Albertville 1992

1. Name the president of France who officially opened these Games.
2. Which famous footballer lit the Olympic cauldron during the opening ceremony?
3. Name either of the two sports that made their Winter Olympic debut in Albertville.
4. With victory in the biathlon (7.5km), Anfisa Reztsova of the Unified Team became the first Winter Olympic champion in two different sports, having won gold in what other sport in 1988?
5. Competitors from which European country won every male cross-country skiing race?
6. In Alpine skiing, Petra Kronberger won both the combined event and the slalom for what nation?
7. Name the American woman who claimed two titles in speed skating.
8. Who defeated Canada 3–1 in the ice hockey final?
9. A traditional power in winter sports, which European country left Albertville with just one medal (a bronze)?
10. The southern hemisphere gained its first medal in Winter Olympic history when Annelise Coberger took a silver in the women's slalom in Alpine skiing. What nation did she represent?

Answers on page 259

Lillehammer 1994

1. What was the name of the King of Norway who officially opened these Games?
2. Name either sport in which professionals were allowed to compete for the first time.
3. Star performer was Norway's John Olav Koss, who claimed three titles, all in world record times, in what sport?
4. The most successful female competitor was Italy's Manuela di Centa, who won five medals in what sport?
5. Myriam Bédard, the winner of both individual events in women's biathlon, represented what nation?
6. In Alpine skiing, Vreni Schneider won a full set of medals for which country?
7. Who recovered from a much publicised assault to gain a silver medal in figure skating?
8. Also in figure skating, Britain's Torvill and Dean finished in what position in the pairs event, leading to criticism of the standards of judging?
9. Which team did Sweden beat in a dramatic penalty shootout in the ice hockey final?
10. What nation placed second in the medal table behind Russia but won the most medals in total?

Answers on page 259

Nagano 1998

1. What was the name of the Emperor of Japan who officially opened these Games?
2. Which sport made its debut as a Winter Olympic medal sport in Nagano?
3. In what sport were women allowed to compete for the first time at a Winter Olympics?
4. Teenage figure skater Tara Lipinski won gold in the ladies' singles representing which country?
5. The outstanding performer here was Norway's Bjørn Dæhlie, who claimed three titles in what sport?
6. In Alpine skiing, which Austrian star recovered from a fall in the men's downhill event to win gold in the super-G and giant slalom?
7. Which East European nation claimed its first ever Winter Olympic title when Ekaterina Dafovska struck gold in the 15 km individual event in biathlon?
8. Which new nation claimed its first title in men's ice hockey by defeating Russia in a closely fought final?
9. In what sport did Germany's Katja Seizinger win two golds?
10. What country in the southern hemisphere won its first individual Winter Olympic medal when Zali Steggall took bronze in the women's slalom in Alpine skiing?

Answers on page 260

Salt Lake City 2002

1. Which prominent politician officially opened these Games?
2. These were the first Games to be held during the term of which president of the IOC?
3. The official theme tune, *Call of the Champions*, was written by which famous composer who celebrated his 70th birthday on the day of the opening ceremony?
4. Which former British colony made its Winter Olympic debut here?
5. The most successful competitor was Norway's Ole Einar Bjørndalen, who won four gold medals in which sport?
6. Samppa Lajunen earned three golds in Nordic combined for what country?
7. Which Asian country won its first two Winter Olympic gold medals when a team member took two titles in speed skating?
8. Australia's Alisa Camplin became first female Winter Olympic champion from the southern hemisphere when she triumphed in what sport?
9. Which country won both the men's and women's titles in ice hockey?
10. Norway topped the medal table with 13 golds, but which fellow European nation won a record number of medals in total?

Answers on page 260

Turin 2006

1. A spectacular opening ceremony featured which famous tenor singing in public for the final time?
2. Name the famous Italian film actress who helped bring the Olympic torch into the stadium.
3. The Olympic flame was lit by Stefania Belmondo, a former Winter Olympic champion for Italy in what sport?
4. The outstanding performer was South Korea's Ahn Hyun-Soo, who won three gold medals and a bronze in which sport?
5. Michael Greis of Germany claimed three titles in what sport?
6. Following her three golds in Salt Lake City, Janica Kostelić became the only woman to win four titles in Alpine skiing with victory in the combined event. Which former Yugoslav republic did she represent?
7. Shani Davis (USA) became the first black male to gain individual gold at a Winter Olympics with victory what sport?
8. Cindy Klaasen won five medals in speed skating for which country?
9. What European team claimed the men's ice hockey title as, for the first time, the USA, Russia and Canada all failed to win a medal?
10. Who was Great Britain's only medallist in Turin?

Answers on page 261

Vancouver 2010

1. A much-used phrase during the Games, what was the name of the programme set up to help Canada win medals?
2. The luger Nodar Kumaritashvili, who was tragically killed in Vancouver while training for the Games, represented which former Soviet republic?
3. Alexandre Bilodeau made history as the first Canadian to win an Olympic title on home soil when he triumphed in what sport?
4. Which female Norwegian cross-country skier was the star performer in Vancouver with five medals including three golds?
5. The winner of two medals (gold, bronze), Lindsay Vonn of the United States competed in five events in which sport?
6. The brothers Andreas and Wolfgang Linger retained their luge doubles title for what country?
7. In ski jumping, Simon Ammann regained the two titles (individual normal hill, individual long hill) that he had first won in 2002. Which European country does he represent?
8. Name the American who won a full set of medals in men's Alpine skiing, including gold in the super combined event.
9. Which team won its third consecutive Olympic title in women's ice hockey?
10. What European nation was runner-up to Canada in the medal table?

Answers on page 261

6. WINTER OLYMPIC SPORTS

Alpine Skiing

1. Which two events in Olympic Alpine skiing are decided on the basis of one run?
2. What nationality was the first female Olympic champion in Alpine skiing?
3. In 1948, Gretchen Fraser became the first non-European to win an Alpine skiing title when she took gold in the slalom. Which nation did she represent?
4. For what European country did Zeno Colo win gold in the men's downhill in 1952?
5. In 1960, which Frenchman changed the sport by becoming the first Olympic champion to use metal skis?
6. Winner of downhill gold in 1972 and silver in 1976, Bernhard Russi competed for what country?
7. Which Austrian star rounded off an outstanding career by winning her first Olympic title in 1980?
8. Name the male Norwegian skier who won five Alpine medals, including one gold, in the period 1994–2006
9. In what event did Italy's Deborah Compagnoni retain her Olympic title at Nagano 1998?
10. In 1998, which British skier competed in a record fifth Olympic downhill event in his final Winter Games?
11. What nationality is Kjetil André Aamod, who in 2006 won a joint-record fourth gold in men's Alpine skiing and a record eighth medal in total?
12. In which Alpine skiing event at Vancouver 2010 were the three medallists separated by a mere 0.09 seconds?

Answers on page 262

Biathlon

1. In individual races, competitors start at intervals of how many seconds?
2. All targets in biathlon are set at a distance of how many metres from the shooters?
3. How many shots does each competitor take in each shooting round of an individual biathlon competition?
4. In what decade was the inaugural Olympic biathlon held?
5. The first Olympic biathlon champion represented which country?
6. In which year did women first compete in biathlon at the Winter Olympics?
7. Which now-defunct nation claimed the first six titles in the men's relay?
8. Magnar Solberg, who retained his 20km title in 1972, represented what nation?
9. Which Norwegian biathlete won a full set of medals (gold, silver, bronze) at the 1984 Games in Sarajevo?
10. What country won both relay events (men's and women's) at Nagano in 1998?
11. In 2010, Lee-Steve Jackson became the first British competitor to qualify for what event in Olympic biathlon?
12. Which German star won two golds in women's biathlon at Vancouver 2010?

Answers on page 262

Bobsleigh

1. In what year did women first compete in Olympic bobsleigh?
2. In which decade did men first compete in two-man bobsleigh at the Winter Games?
3. What European country took a gold and two silvers in bobsleigh at the 1956 Games in Cortina?
4. Which East European nation won its only medal in Winter Olympic history when taking bronze in the two-man event at Grenoble 1968?
5. Which now-defunct country claimed both titles at the 1976 Games in Innsbruck?
6. What nation won its final bobsleigh title (four-man bob) at Calgary 1988?
7. A pair from which European country retained their two-man bob title in 1994?
8. In 1998, teams from what two countries were both awarded gold medals in the two-man event after recording exactly the same time for their four runs?
9. Who became the first black competitor to win a gold medal at the Winter Olympics when she teamed up with Jill Bakken to win the two-woman event for the USA in 2002?
10. What nation achieved a clean sweep of bobsleigh golds at Turin 2006?
11. At Vancouver 2010, which British pair went into the two-woman bob as world champions but withdrew from the event after their sled crossed the line on its side on their second run?
12. Teams from which country finished first and second in the two-woman event in 2010?

Answers on page 263

Cross-country (Nordic) Skiing

1. Skiers from which country took all three medals in the 15km event in 1948?
2. In 1952, the inaugural Winter Olympic cross country event for women, the 10km, saw all three medals go to what nation?
3. Which Swedish skier ended his outstanding career at the 1964 Games after winning nine Olympic medals including four golds?
4. At Grenoble in 1968, Franco Nones became the first skier from a non-Nordic nation to win Olympic gold in cross country skiing with victory in the 30km event. What country did he represent?
5. In 1976, which American skier won silver in the 30km event using a new 'skating' technique?
6. At Lake Placid in 1980, in what event did Sweden's Thomas Wassberg defeat Finland's Juha Meito by 0.01 seconds, the closest margin of victory in Winter Olympic history?
7. Which Norwegian skier crossed the line backwards to celebrate his country winning gold in the men's relay in 1992?
8. Name the Russian winner of three golds and a silver at Lillehammer 1994.
9. In 2002, in what event did Norway's Thomas Alsgaard and Frode Estil dead-heat, each being awarded a gold medal?
10. Andrus Veerpalu, who retained his 15km title in 2006, was the first Winter Olympic champion from which Baltic state?
11. Which women's event was introduced at Turin 2006?
12. In what event at Vancouver 2010 did Petter Northug (Norway) beat Germany's Axel Teichmann by a mere 0.3 seconds?

Answers on page 263

Curling

1. How many players are in a curling team and how many stones do they each deliver in each 'end'?
2. What name is given to the ring of circles towards which play is directed?
3. In which decade was a curling competition first held at the Winter Olympics?
4. In 1924, the first Olympic competition was won by a Great Britain team selected from a curling club in which Scottish city?
5. What nation took gold in the women's event when curling was reintroduced as a medal sport to the Olympics in 1998?
6. Who did the Great Britain women's team defeat to take gold in Salt Lake City in 2002?
7. Which European nation won its first curling gold in Winter Olympic history with victory in the men's event in 2002?
8. At Turin 2006, which team did Great Britain men's team lose to in the bronze medal match?
9. What European nation took its first curling medal with a silver in the men's event in 2006?
10. Which country retained its women's title at the 2010 Games in Vancouver?
11. In 2010, which nation became the first from Asia to win an Olympic medal in curling?
12. Who was the 19-year-old 'skip' (captain) of the Great Britain women's curling team in Vancouver?

Answers on page 264

Figure Skating

1. Held at the 1908 Summer Olympics, the first Olympic figure skating competition saw which British skater win gold in the ladies' singles and, with her husband, bronze in the pairs?
2. Karl Schäfer, who retained his men's singles crown in 1936, competed for which nation?
3. Champion in St Moritz in 1948, Barbara Ann Scott remains the only woman from what country to win an individual Olympic gold medal in figure skating?
4. Which American skater won the 1956 ladies singles title only two weeks after sustaining a serious injury in practice?
5. A bronze medallist in 1960, Donald Jackson of Canada later became the first skater to land what jump in competition?
6. Name the Italian coach who guided both John Curry (GBR) and Dorothy Hamill (USA) to figure skating titles in 1976.
7. Also in 1976, what dangerous manoeuvre was first completed in competition by American figure skater Terry Kubicka?
8. At the 1988 Calgary Games, what were the surnames of the two skaters involved in the 'Battle of the Brians'?
9. In 1992, Midori Ito (USA) became the first woman to perform what manoeuvre in Olympic competition?
10. At Salt Lake City in 2002, which American star was hot favourite for the ladies' singles title but had to settle for a bronze medal after falling during her long programme?
11. In 2006, married couple Povilas Vanagas and Margarita Drobiazko became the first figure skaters to compete at five Olympics. What Baltic state did they represent in Turin?
12. On her way to earning a silver medal in the ladies' singles in Vancouver, which Japanese skater became the first woman to land a triple axel in an Olympic short programme?

Answers on page 264

Freestyle Skiing

1. What are the three disciplines in freestyle skiing at the Winter Games?
2. In which decade did freestyle skiing make its debut at the Winter Olympics as a demonstration sport?
3. Later renamed Acroski, which freestyle skiing discipline was a demonstration sport at the Winter Games but is no longer a competitive event?
4. What European country took the first two places in the inaugural men's moguls in 1992?
5. Winner of the women's moguls in 1994, Lina Cheryazová is the only Winter Olympic champion in any sport from which central Asian republic?
6. What country dominated this sport at Nagano 1998, taking three of the four titles on offer?
7. Kari Traa, who collected a full set of Olympic medals in the women's moguls in the period 1998–2006, competed for which European nation?
8. On the way to winning the men's aerials competition in 2002, Aleš Valenta of the Czech Republic performed a triple back flip with how many twists?
9. What Asian country claimed its first Winter Olympic title in freestyle skiing in 2006?
10. Michael Schmid, who in 2010 became the inaugural Olympic champion in men's ski cross, represents which nation?
11. At Vancouver 2010, Alexei Grishin won the men's aerials for what former Soviet republic?
12. Also in 2010, Lydia Lassila won the women's aerials representing which southern hemisphere country?

Answers on page 265

Ice Hockey

1. In what year was the first Olympic ice hockey tournament held?
2. Which country won the first four Olympic titles in men's ice hockey?
3. In 1956, which nation marked its debut in Olympic ice hockey by winning all seven matches as it comfortably took gold?
4. What country's ice hockey side were nicknamed the 'Team of Destiny' after their surprise triumph at the 1960 Games?
5. Which Midwestern university provided the coach (Herb Brooks) and nine of the USA squad that took a shock Olympic gold in 1980?
6. The top three leading goalscorers in 1980 all competed for which East European nation?
7. The outcome of the 1994 men's final is the only one in Olympic history to be decided by what method?
8. Which nation won the inaugural women's title in 1998?
9. In 2006, what European team lost to Canada's women by an Olympic record score of 16–0?
10. Name the scorer of the winning goal as Canada defeated the USA in a dramatic men's ice hockey final in 2010.
11. In the women's competition in Vancouver, which European team was beaten 9–1 by the USA in a one-sided semi-final?
12. In 2010, a player from what country became the all-time leader for points scored in Olympic ice hockey?

Answers on page 265

Luge

1. Placings in the two-seater event (doubles) are decided on the basis of two runs per pair, but how many runs feature in the singles events?
2. Which Polish-born British slider was tragically killed in practice for the inaugural Olympic luge competition in 1964?
3. What European country achieved a clean sweep of the medals in the singles in 1964?
4. The only non-German speaking Olympic champion in luge, Vera Zozuja competed for which nation when taking gold in the women's singles in 1980?
5. George Tucker, who finished last in the men's singles in 1984, was the first Winter Olympian from which Central American country?
6. What was the surname of the three Italian brothers who all gained medals at Lillehammer in 1994?
7. Which German slider completed an unprecedented hat-trick of men's singles titles at Nagano 1998?
8. In the period 1998–2010, Armin Zöggeler won two golds and two bronzes in the men's singles for what country?
9. Name the German slider who retained her women's singles crown at Turin 2006.
10. For which country did brothers Andreas and Wolfgang Linger claim the doubles title in 2006?
11. Both singles events at Vancouver 2010 were won by competitors from what European country?
12. Brother Andris and Juris Šics won silver in the doubles in 2010 for which Baltic state?

Answers on page 266

Nordic Combined

1. What are the two disciplines in Nordic combined?
2. In which year did Nordic combined make its debut at the Winter Olympics?
3. Which nation achieved a clean sweep of the medals in the each of the first four individual competitions?
4. Competitors from what country finished first and second in the individual event at St Moritz in 1948?
5. In 1960, Georg Thoma became the first non-Scandinavian to win this event. Which nation did he represent?
6. Runner-up in the individual event in 1968, Alois Kälin was the first competitor from what European nation to gain a Winter Olympic medal in Nordic skiing?
7. Name the East German star who claimed his third consecutive individual title in 1980.
8. What nation were the winners of the inaugural team event at Calgary 1988?
9. The first non-European Olympic champions in Nordic combined, which Asian country won the first team event at Albertville in 1992 and retained its title two years later?
10. In 2002, which Finnish star achieved an unprecedented haul of three golds in Nordic combined at the same Olympics?
11. Star performer at Turin 2006 was Felix Gottwald, who took two golds and a silver for what country?
12. At Vancouver 2010, the sprint and individual events of 7.5 km and 15 km, respectively, were replaced by two individual events over what distance?

Answers on page 266

Short-track Speed Skating

1. What is the shortest distance for races in short-track speed skating at the Olympics?
2. How many skaters usually compete in each race?
3. What is the minimum age limit for competitors in this sport?
4. Short-track speed skating made its Winter Olympic debut, as a demonstration sport, in what decade?
5. Winner of a bronze in the men's 500m event in 1992, Nicky Gooch remains what nation's only Winter Olympic medallist in this sport?
6. Name the Korean star who retained his men's 1000m title at Lillehammer in 1994.
7. Which event was introduced at the 2002 Games in Salt Lake City?
8. In a dramatic climax to the men's 1000m final in 2002, the leading trio fell just short of the finishing line, allowing Steven Bradbury to come through and become the first ever Winter Olympic champion from what nation?
9. In the women's competition, which country claimed its fourth consecutive 3000m relay title in 2006?
10. With two medals at Vancouver 2010 taking his career total to eight, Apolo Anton Ohno became the most decorated Winter Olympian for which nation?
11. Charles Hamelin won two golds in 2010 competing for what country?
12. Name the female Chinese skater who won three golds in Vancouver.

Answers on page 267

Skeleton

1. In which decade was a skeleton competition first held at a Winter Olympics?
2. As from 2010, placings are decided on the combined times of how many runs?
3. Which American slider won his second Olympic silver medal in the skeleton in 1948, 20 years after winning his first at the age of 19?
4. Name the famous Italian sledder who claimed the men's title at St Moritz in 1948.
5. Which country had three men finish in the top seven in 1948?
6. What nation achieved a 1-2 in the inaugural women's event at Salt Lake City in 2002?
7. Name the female British sledder who gained a bronze medal in 2002.
8. For which European nation did Clifton Wrottesley place fourth in the men's event in 2002?
9. At Turin 2006, Gregor Stähli gained his second successive bronze competing for what country?
10. Name the British sledder who gained a silver medal in the women's event in 2006.
11. For which Baltic state did Martin Dukurs take a silver medal at Vancouver 2010?
12. In the women's event in 2010, competitors from which country placed second and third as Great Britain's Amy Williams took gold?

Answers on page 267

172

Ski Jumping

1. Winner of a bronze medal in the inaugural Winter Olympic ski jumping competition in 1924, Anders Haugen represented which nation?
2. What was the surname of the Norwegian brothers Asbjørn, Birger and Sigmund, who competed in ski jumping at the Winter Olympics between 1928 and 1948?
3. Giving his name to a ski jumping technique, which Swiss star introduced a new style of jumping at the 1956 Games in Cortina?
4. At Grenoble 1968, Winter Olympic history was made as two jumpers exceeded what distance in the men's large hill event for the first time?
5. Successful in the normal hill event in 1972, what nationality was the first non-European Olympic champion in ski jumping?
6. Name the Finnish jumper who won four gold medals in the period 1984–1988.
7. At Calgary 1988, Sweden's Jan Boklöv introduced a controversial style of jumping named after which letter of the alphabet?
8. What European nation took four of the top six places, including first and second, in the normal hill event in 1992?
9. Name the winning nation in the large hill team event in both 1994 and 2002.
10. Which Polish former world champion was runner-up in the large hill event in both 2002 and 2010?
11. Which Austrian ace won two golds in 2006 and one in 2010?
12. At Vancouver 2010, which Swiss star reclaimed the two individual titles he had first won in 2002?

Answers on page 268

Snowboarding

1. At Nagano 1998, the inaugural Olympic snowboarding competition was mired in controversy after the winner of the men's giant slalom was disqualified for failing a drug test – and then reinstated. What was his name?
2. The winner of the first women's giant slalom, Karine Ruby, represented which nation?
3. For what European country did Gian Simmen win the men's halfpipe in 1998?
4. Which country achieved a clean sweep of the medals in the men's halfpipe event at Salt Lake City in 2002?
5. Bronze medallist in the men's halfpipe in 2002, Chris Klug (USA) had received a transplant for which body organ only 18 months earlier?
6. For which European nation did Lidia Trettel earn a bronze in the women's parallel giant slalom in 2002?
7. What event was introduced at the 2006 Games in Turin?
8. Name the Swiss star who retained his parallel giant slalom title in 2006.
9. The 2010 snowboarding competition was held at which ski resort near Vancouver?
10. Nicknamed the 'Flying Tomato' for his long red hair, which American ace retained his men's halfpipe crown in 2010?
11. Which American snowboarder retained his snowboard cross title in Vancouver?
12. What European nation won its first Winter Olympic medal outside of ice skating when Nicolien Sauerbreij won gold in the parallel giant slalom in 2010?

Answers on page 268

Speed Skating

1. Which speed skating event at the 1928 Games was controversially abandoned because of bad weather, resulting in no medals being awarded?
2. Who became the first American to win two golds at the same Winter Olympics when claiming two speed skating titles at the 1932 Games in Lake Placid?
3. What event did Norway's Finn Helgesen win in Olympic record time at the 1948 Games in St Moritz?
4. Which event in 1956 resulted in a dead-heat, both men being awarded gold medals?
5. At the 1960 Games, which male Norwegian skater won 10000m gold in world record time, becoming the was the first skater to break the 16-minute barrier?
6. In what event at the 1968 Games did three women tie for the silver medal?
7. Name the male Dutch skater who won three golds at the 1972 Games in Sapporo.
8. Which Swedish star retained his 500m title in 1988?
9. Name the American female skater who collected five Olympic golds in the period 1988–1994.
10. In 2002, which German star claimed her third successive 5000m title and her first at 3000m, setting world records in both events?
11. What Asian country gained silver and bronze medals in the women's 500m event in 2006?
12. Which nation topped the speed skating medal table at Vancouver 2010?

Answers on page 269

175

7. WINTER OLYMPICS NUMBERS

Part 1 – How many?

1. How many gold medals have Great Britain won at the Winter Olympics?
   (a) 6
   (b) 7
   (c) 8
   (d) 9

2. How many gold medals did the Soviet Union win when competing at the Winter Olympics between 1952 and 1988?
   (a) 58
   (b) 68
   (c) 78
   (d) 88

3. The freestyle skiing discipline of Aeriels is the 'highest' event at the Winter Olympics, with competitors often jumping how many metres into the air?
   (a) 6
   (b) 10
   (c) 14
   (d) 18

4. How many women competed in the first Winter Olympics at Chamonix in 1924?
   (a) 3
   (b) 13
   (c) 43
   (d) 73

Answers on page 270

5. How many nations competed in ice hockey at the 1932 Games in Lake Placid?
   (a) 4
   (b) 8
   (c) 12
   (d) 16

6. What was the estimated crowd for the ski jumping at the 1952 Games in Oslo?
   (a) 50,000
   (b) 100,000
   (c) 150,000
   (d) 200,000

7. In 1955, Squaw Valley in California was chosen to host the 1960 Games. How many inhabitants did it have at the time?
   (a) 1
   (b) 101
   (c) 1001
   (d) 10001

8. In figure skating at the 1984 Games, how many perfect 6.0 scores for artistic impression did Torvill and Dean achieve in their free dance routine?
   (a) 3
   (b) 5
   (c) 7
   (d) 9

Answers on page 270

9. How many nations made their Winter Olympic debut at the 1994 Games in Lillehammer?
   (a) 5
   (b) 8
   (c) 11
   (d) 14

10. How many events were contested at Vancouver 2010?
    (a) 76
    (b) 86
    (c) 96
    (d) 106

11. In ski jumping in Vancouver, two men leapt a joint Olympic record in the large hill individual event. How far in metres did they jump?
    (a) 119
    (b) 129
    (c) 139
    (d) 149

12. The USA set a new record by winning how many medals at Vancouver 2010?
    (a) 35
    (b) 37
    (c) 39
    (d) 41

Answers on page 270

Part 2 – A Question of Age

1. The oldest champion in Winter Olympic history, what age was Robin Welsh win he helped Great Britain claim the curling title in 1924?
   (a) 46
   (b) 50
   (c) 54
   (d) 58

2. Both the oldest competitor and medallist in Winter Olympic history, what age was Carl Kronlund when he helped Sweden win silver in curling at the 1924 Games?
   (a) 50
   (b) 53
   (c) 56
   (d) 59

3. How old was Ethel Muckelt when she won a bronze medal for Great Britain in figure skating in 1924?
   (a) 16
   (b) 24
   (c) 30
   (d) 38

4. The youngest ever female competitor at either the Winter or Summer Olympics, how old was Britain's Cecilia Colledge when she competed in figure skating in 1932?
   (a) 10
   (b) 11
   (c) 12
   (d) 13

Answers on page 270

5. One of the oldest Winter Olympic medallists, how old was Belgium's Max Houben when he took silver in the four-man bobsleigh in 1948?
   (a) 41
   (b) 45
   (c) 49
   (d) 53

6. The youngest male Winter Olympian, what age was East Germany's Jan Hoffman when he competed in figure skating at the 1968 Grenoble Games?
   (a) 12
   (b) 14
   (c) 16
   (d) 18

7. The oldest female champion in an individual event at the Winter Olympics, how old was Christina Bass-Kaiser (NED) when successful in speed skating in 1972?
   (a) 31
   (b) 33
   (c) 35
   (d) 37

8. The youngest male champion in Winter Olympic history, how old was Finland's Toni Nieminen when he won the first of two golds in ski jumping in 1992?
   (a) 15
   (b) 16
   (c) 17
   (d) 18

Answers on page 270

9. In 1994, Kim Yun-Mi became the youngest ever Olympic champion when she helped South Korea to victory in the 3000m relay in short-track speed skating. How old was she?
(a) 13
(b) 14
(c) 15
(d) 16

10. The youngest gold medallist in an individual event, how old was figure skater Tara Lipinski (USA) when she won the ladies' singles title at Nagano 1998?
(a) 13
(b) 14
(c) 15
(d) 16

11. The oldest female competitor in Winter Olympic history, how old was Anne Abernathy (US Virgin Islands) when she took part in the luge in 2002?
(a) 42
(b) 44
(c) 46
(d) 48

12. The oldest individual champion in Winter Olympic history, what age was Canada's Duff Gibson when he won gold in the men's skeleton in 2006?
(a) 39
(b) 42
(c) 45
(d) 48

Answers on page 270

Part 3 – Name the Year

1. At which year's Winter Olympics did the number of competitors first exceed the 1000 mark?
   (a) 1956
   (b) 1964
   (c) 1972
   (d) 1980

2. In which year did Canada first refuse to take part in ice hockey at the Winter Olympics?
   (a) 1952
   (b) 1964
   (c) 1972
   (d) 1980

3. At what year's Games did the number of *female* competitors first pass the 1000 mark?
   (a) 1998
   (b) 2002
   (c) 2006
   (d) 2010

4. In which year did women first compete in speed skating at the Winter Olympics?
   (a) 1956
   (b) 1960
   (c) 1964
   (d) 1968

Answers on page 271

5. In what year did snowboarding make its Winter Olympic debut?
   (a) 1992
   (b) 1994
   (c) 1998
   (d) 2002

6. In which year did women first compete in ice hockey at the Winter Olympics?
   (a) 1992
   (b) 1994
   (c) 1998
   (d) 2002

7. Before returning to the Winter Olympic schedule in 2002, in what year had skeleton previously been a medal sport at the Games?
   (a) 1948
   (b) 1956
   (c) 1960
   (d) 1964

8. Which year's Games were the first to welcome more than 2000 competitors?
   (a) 1988
   (b) 1992
   (c) 1994
   (d) 1998

Answers on page 271

9. What year's Winter Olympics were the first to be televised?
   (a) 1948
   (b) 1952
   (c) 1956
   (d) 1960

10. In which year did a British man last win an individual title at the Winter Olympics?
    (a) 1976
    (b) 1980
    (c) 1984
    (d) 1988

11. When was the last time the Summer and Winter Olympics were held in the same year?
    (a) 1984
    (b) 1988
    (c) 1992
    (d) 1996

12. When was the last time the Summer and Winter Olympics were held *in the same country* in the same year?
    (a) 1928
    (b) 1936
    (c) 1952
    (d) 1960

Answers on page 271

Part 4 – Placings and scores

1. In men's curling, by what score did Great Britain beat France on their way to winning gold at the 1924 Games?
   (a) 16–4
   (b) 26–4
   (c) 36–4
   (d) 46–4

2. In 1936, Great Britain clinched the ice hockey title after drawing with the United States in their last group match. What was the final score?
   (a) 0–0
   (b) 1–1
   (c) 2–2
   (d) 3–3

3. Later the coach of several Olympic champions, Italy's Carlo Fassi achieved what placing in men's figure skating in 1952?
   (a) 4th
   (b) 6th
   (c) 8th
   (d) 10th

4. In 1964, in what position did future Olympic champion Jean-Claude Killy finish in the giant slalom event in Alpine skiing?
   (a) 3rd
   (b) 5th
   (c) 7th
   (d) 9th

Answers on page 271

5. In ice hockey, by what score did the USSR defeat Poland in a
   final round match in 1972?
   (a) 10–1
   (b) 12–1
   (c) 14–1
   (d) 16–1

6. By what score did the United States beat the Soviet Union in
   an epic match ice hockey match at the 1980 Games?
   (a) 2–1
   (b) 3–2
   (c) 4–3
   (d) 5–4

7. In what position did Jayne Torvill and Christopher Dean finish
   in the pairs event in figure skating at Lake Placid in 1980?
   (a) 5th
   (b) 7th
   (c) 9th
   (d) 11th

8. By what score did the USA beat Canada in the inaugural
   women's ice hockey final in 1998?
   (a) 2–1
   (b) 3–2
   (c) 3–1
   (d) 3–2

Answers on page 271

9. By what score did Great Britain beat Switzerland in the 2002 women's curling final?
   (a) 3–2
   (b) 4–3
   (c) 5–4
   (d) 6–5

10. In short-track speed skating, where did Great Britain's Jon Eley place in the 500m event at Turin 2006?
    (a) 5th
    (b) 7th
    (c) 9th
    (d) 11th

11. The best performing Asian country at Vancouver 2010, in what position did South Korea place in the medal table?
    (a) 5th
    (b) 7th
    (c) 9th
    (d) 11th

12. By what score did Canada beat the USA in the 2010 men's ice hockey final?
    (a) 2–1
    (b) 3–2
    (c) 4–3
    (d) 5–4

Answers on page 271

8. WINTER OLYMPICS MIXED BAG

Part 1 – First Things First

1. Who was the first competitor from Great Britain to claim an individual title at the Winter Olympics?
2. Billy Fiske, who won bobsleigh gold in the USA four-man team of 1932, had the distinction of being the first American to join which branch of the British armed services in WWII?
3. What year's Winter Olympics were the first to have a dedicated 'village' for the competitors?
4. At Grenoble 1968, Alois Schloder became the first Olympian to test positive for a banned substance – but was still allowed to compete in ice hockey. Which nation did he represent?
5. What figure skating event was introduced to the Olympics at the 1976 Games in Innsbruck?
6. Name the west African nation that made its Winter Olympic debut at Sarajevo in 1984.
7. In 1992, who became the first person to win the same Alpine skiing event twice?
8. Jarome Iginla of Canada became the first black male Winter Olympic champion when winning gold in what sport in 2002?
9. In 2010, Haralds Silovs became the first person in Olympic history to compete in short track (1500m) and long track (5000m) speed skating, and the first to take part in two different disciplines on the same day. What European nation does he represent?
10. Name either of the two East European nations that gained their first Winter Olympic gold medals at Vancouver 2010.

Answers on page 272

Part 2 – Famous Winter Olympians

1. Which female Norwegian figure skater won three Olympic titles (1928–36) and later pursued an acting career, becoming one of the highest paid stars in Hollywood?
2. After retiring from competitive skiing in 1968, which multiple Olympic champion drove in the Paris-Dakar rally and had a short career as a film actor?
3. Name the figure skater who received 35,000 love letters after winning gold at the 1984 Games in Sarajevo.
4. What is the real name of 'Eddie the Eagle', the British competitor who gained widespread media attention for his hapless performance at the 1988 Calgary Games?
5. Prince Albert of Monaco competed in what sport at all five Winter Olympics between 1988 and 2002?
6. Which famous Alpine skier took up motor racing after retiring from winter sports and in 1990 won a round of the prestigious European Touring Car Championship?
7. Nicknamed 'Schmirler the Curler', who captained the Canada women's curling team to victory at Nagano in 1998 – but died from cancer only two years later at the age of 36?
8. Which British woman competed in Alpine skiing and speed skating at the Winter Olympics and later had a career as a motor racing driver?
9. Amy Williams, the 2010 skeleton champion, was granted the freedom of which English city in June 2010?
10. Now a Conservative peer, Lord Glentoran won a gold medal at the Winter Olympics competing under what name?

Answers on page 272

Part 3 – Record breakers

1. What nation has won the most gold most medals at the Winter Olympics?
2. A legend of cross-country skiing, which competitor has won both the most golds and the most medals in total?
3. Name either of the competitors to have won a female joint-record of six Winter Olympic golds?
4. Identify either of the women (both cross-country skiers) who have won a female joint-record of 10 medals at the Winter Games.
5. The winner of nine medals, including five golds, speed skater Claudia Pechstein is which country's most successful Winter Olympian?
6. The record score in Olympic ice hockey came in 1924 when Canada beat what central European nation 33–0?
7. In what sport did Aleksandr Tikhonov (USSR) win a record four consecutive gold medals between 1968 and 1980?
8. Aged 33 when she won gold in 1972, Christina Baas-Kaiser of the Netherlands is the oldest woman to win an indvidual Winter Olympic title. In what sport was she successful?
9. When claiming a downhill title in the 1980s, which Alpine skier recorded the fastest average speed in Olympic history during a downhill race?
10. What was the record number of gold medals won by Canada at Vancouver 2010?

Answers on page 273

Part 4 – Trivia Teasers

1. In what sport did American brothers Jennison and John Heaton win Olympic gold and silver medals, respectively, in 1928?
2. How did Giuliana Chenal-Minuzzo make history at the opening ceremony of the 1952 Games in Oslo?
3. Which famous company was responsible for producing both the opening and closing ceremonies of the 1960 Games in Squaw Valley?
4. Which multiple Winter Olympic champion was born in Cornwall in 1964?
5. In 1968, three women's luge teams from East Germany were disqualified for what illegal activity?
6. Name the Austrian skier who was banned from the 1972 Winter Olympics after he was accused of being a professional.
7. What was the name of the film made about the appearance of a Jamaican men's bobsleigh team at the 1988 Calgary Games?
8. Winner of a bronze in the men's sprint in cross-country skiing in 2002, Italy's Cristian Zorzi dressed in a black cape and mask at the medal ceremony with reference to his being nicknamed after which fictional character?
9. An Olympic medallist in 2010, which female German skeleton sledder is nicknamed the 'Ice Tiger'?
10. Two polar bears named *Hidy* and *Howdu* were the official mascots of which Winter Olympics?

Answers on page 273

PART C –
ANSWERS

9. SUMMER OLYMPICS ANSWERS

1. Summer Olympics History

Part 1 – Overview
1. Olympia
2. Much Wenlock (The Wenlock Olympian Society Annual Games are still held today)
3. Pierre Frédy, Baron de Coubertin
4. Athens
5. Melbourne (1956)
6. 1924 (Paris)
7. Tokyo (1964)
8. 1908, 1948
9. Switzerland
10. Fencing

Part 2 – Recent history (1980–2012)
1. The Soviet Union's invasion of Afghanistan (1979)
2. Carl Lewis
3. Basketball
4. Beach volleyball
5. Cathy Freeman
6. 800m, 1500m
7. Eight
8. *Inspire a Generation*
9. Rio de Janeiro
10. Istanbul, Madrid, Tokyo

The Modern Games

Athens 1896
 1. King George I
 2. Discus throw, marathon
 3. Bronze
 4. Hop, step and jump (now triple jump)
 5. Wrestling
 6. Fencing
 7. Tennis (singles, men's doubles)
 8. Marathon
 9. Swimming
10. USA (11 golds)

Paris 1900
 1. The *Exposition Universelle* (World's Fair)
 2. Sailing (mixed 1-2 tonne class; crew member on father's yacht)
 3. Grass (at the Croix-Catelan Stadium)
 4. Alvin Kraenzlein (60m, 110mH, 200mH, long jump)
 5. Ray Ewry
 6. Luxembourg
 7. Le Havre
 8. The *Bois de Boulogne*
 9. Canada
10. Rugby (union)

St Louis 1904

1. Chicago
2. Theodore Roosevelt
3. Gymnastics
4. New York City
5. Jim Lightbody (also won 800m, 2590m steeplechase)
6. Golf
7. Canada (their women's team won bronze in 2012)
8. Swimming
9. He travelled by car
10. Cuba (4 golds)

Athens 1906 (Intercalated Games)

1. The Parade of Nations
2. Panathinaiko (or Panathenaic) Stadium
3. The United States
4. Shooting
5. Finland (Verner Järvinen, discus throw – Greek style)
6. Paul Pilgrim
7. 5 miles
8. Greece
9. Eric Lemming
10. Martin Sheridan (USA)

London 1908

1. King Edward VII
2. White City stadium
3. Hockey
4. Boxing (five weight divisions; only non-British medallist was Australia's Snowy Baker, who won a middleweight silver)
5. Dorando Pietri
6. Sir Arthur Conan Doyle
7. Football
8. Figure skating
9. Charles Daniels
10. Sweden (8 golds)

Stockholm 1912

1. Egypt
2. Portugal (Francisco Lázaro)
3. Boxing (illegal at the time in Sweden)
4. Diving, swimming
5. Jim Thorpe (USA)
6. 800m (1 min 51.9 secs)
7. 1500m
8. Sailing (6m class)
9. Denmark
10. South Africa

Antwerp 1920

1. The Olympic Oath (taken during the opening ceremony)
2. Figure skating, ice hockey
3. Shooting
4. Albert Hill
5. Charley Paddock
6. Diving (3m springboard)
7. Brazil (30m military pistol)
8. Sailing (Belgium, Netherlands). The final two races in the 12-foot dinghy event were held in the Netherlands, as both entrants were Dutch.
9. Suzanne Lenglen
10. Finland (gained independence from Russia in 1917)

Paris 1924

1. *Citius, Altius, Fortius* (Faster, Higher, Stronger)
2. Stade Colombe
3. Harold Abrahams (100m), Eric Liddell (400m)
4. Fencing
5. High jump
6. Ville Ritola (Paavo Nurmi won five golds)
7. Johnny Weissmuller (USA), played 'Tarzan' in films
8. Polo (men's team competition)
9. Diving (men's springboard event)
10. Hazel Wightman (Wightman Cup)

Amsterdam 1928

1. Gymnastics
2. Discus
3. Triple jump
4. Canada
5. Hammer
6. India
7. Uruguay (beat Argentina 2–1 after a 1–1 draw)
8. Sailing (8m)
9. Gymnastics (women's team event)
10. Germany (10 golds)

Los Angeles 1932

1. Vice President of the United States
2. A hotel (The Chapman Park Hotel on Wilshire Boulevard)
3. Colombia
4. Long Beach
5. Photo-finish equipment
6. 4x100m
7. USA
8. Wrestling
9. Water polo
10. Swimming (men's 4x200m freestyle relay)

Berlin 1936

1. Spain (although the People's Olympiad was cancelled because of the outbreak of the Spanish Civil War that year)
2. For being Jewish
3. Torch relay (starting from Olympia, Greece)
4. 100,000
5. Decathlon
6. (Carl Ludwig) 'Luz' Long
7. 1500 metres (3 mins 47.8 secs)
8. Cycling
9. Swimming
10. Gymnastics

London 1948

1. Malta (won the George Cross in World War II)
2. John Mark
3. Rowing (2 golds), sailing (1 gold)
4. Gymnastics (men's)
5. High jump
6. Sri Lanka (then Ceylon)
7. Jamaica
8. Fencing (women's individual foil)
9. Norwegian
10. Matt Busby

Helsinki 1952
1. Soviet Union (had competed as Russia in 1912)
2. Hannes Kolehmainen
3. Marjorie Jackson
4. Luxembourg
5. Equestrian (individual dressage)
6. Diving (10m platform)
7. Ingemar Johansson
8. Denmark
9. *Foxhunter* (team jumping event; ridden by Harry Llewellyn)
10. Germany (7 silver, 17 bronze)

Melbourne 1956
1. The Soviet Union's invasion of Hungary (Nov 1956)
2. Stockholm (Sweden)
3. The Duke of Edinburgh
4. 1500m
5. Shirley de la Hunty (née Strickland)
6. Boxing
7. East Germany
8. Swedish
9. Equestrian (dressage)
10. All the competitors entering the stadium together (rather than marching in teams as in the opening ceremony).

Rome 1960
1. The Marathon
2. The Bay of Naples
3. Gymnastics
4. Don Thompson (50km walk)
5. Herb Elliott
6. Wilma Rudolph (100m, 200m, 4x100m)
7. Pakistan (won 1–0)
8. Cassius Clay (later Muhammad Ali)
9. Swimming
10. Greece (Prince Constantine; ruled as Constantine II, 1964–73)

Tokyo 1964
1. Emperor Hirohito
2. Hiroshima (6 August 1945)
3. Judo, volleyball
4. Peter Snell
5. Bob Hayes
6. Long jump (6.76m)
7. Swimming (200m women's breaststroke)
8. Joe Frazier
9. Wrestling (Greco-Roman, featherweight)
10. South Africa (banned because of its *apartheid* policies)

Mexico City 1968
1. The Tlatelolco massacre
2. First woman to light the Olympic Cauldron in the stadium
3. Acapulco
4. Dick Fosbury (USA), hence 'Fosbury flop'
5. Bob Beamon (long jump)
6. David Hemery (400m hurdles)
7. Gymnastics
8. Swimming (200, 400 and 800m freestyle)
9. Fencing
10. Japan (11 golds)

Munich 1972
1. Rhodesia
2. 'Black September'
3. Archery (last held in 1920), handball (1936)
4. Shane Gould
5. Valery Borzov
6. Pentathlon
7. Kenya
8. Richard Meade (individual and team three-day eventing)
9. Wrestling (Freestyle, +100 kg category)
10. Netherlands

Montreal 1976
1. New Zealand
2. Basketball, handball
3. Nadia Comăneci
4. 200m breaststroke
5. Hungary
6. Tatyana Kazankina
7. Alberto Juantorena (Cuba)
8. Equestrian
9. Shooting (silver, small bore rifle event)
10. Weightlifting

Moscow 1980
1. President Leonid Brezhnev
2. Tallinn (then USSR, now Estonia)
3. Allan Wells
4. Miruts Yifter ('Yifter the Shifter')
5. Teofilio Stevenson
6. Canoeing
7. Rica Reinisch (100/200m backstroke, 4x100m medley)
8. 100m breaststroke
9. Czechoslovakia
10. *Misha*

Los Angeles 1984
1. He flew in by jet pack
2. Athletics (decathlon, 1960)
3. Synchronised swimming, rhythmic gymnastics
4. Mary Lou Retton
5. Valerie Brisco-Hooks
6. Portugal
7. Shooting (50m pistol)
8. Virginia Holgate (later Leng): team silver, individual bronze
9. The Rose Bowl
10. Romania

Seoul 1988
1. Nagoya
2. Taekwondo
3. Tennis
4. Florence Griffith-Joyner (100m, 200m, 4x100m)
5. Carl Lewis (USA)
6. Peter Elliott
7. Judo
8. Rowing
9. Sailing
10. East Germany (37 golds)

Barcelona 1992

1. He lit the flame in the cauldron by firing an arrow into it.
2. Lithuania
3. *Sagrada Familia* church
4. Swimming
5. 400m hurdles (46.78 secs)
6. Cuba
7. Kieran Perkins
8. Jennifer Capriati (USA)
9. Equestrian (team dressage event)
10. Synchronised swimming

Atlanta 1996

1. Savannah
2. Swimming
3. Michael Johnson (19.32 WR, 43.49 OR)
4. Donovan Bailey
5. Steve Redgrave & Matthew Pinsent (men's coxless pairs)
6. Cycling (women's road race)
7. Andre Agassi (USA)
8. Neil Broad
9. Argentina
10. Equestrian

Sydney 2000
1. Afghanistan
2. Cathy Freeman
3. Cycling
4. Discus
5. Haile Gebrselassie
6. Switzerland
7. Wrestling (Greco-Roman, super heavyweight division, 130kg)
8. Colombia
9. Denise Lewis (heptathlon)
10. Sailing (3 golds)

Athens 2004
1. Olympia
2. Archery (the marathon also ended there)
3. 110m hurdles
4. Hicham El Guerrouj (Morocco)
5. Slovenia
6. Chile (men's singles/doubles)
7. Israel
8. Amir Khan (lightweight division)
9. Argentina
10. Diving (Synchronised 3m springboard, Nikolas Siaranidis & Thomas Bimas)

Beijing 2008

Part 1
1. Toronto
2. Gymnastics
3. The Bird's Nest Stadium, The Water Cube
4. Hong Kong
5. Swimming (10km open water)
6. Kenenisa Bekele (men's), Tirunesh Dibaba (women's)
7. Sudan
8. 3000m Steeplechase (WR of 8:58.81)
9. Yelena Isinbayeva (RUS)
10. Walter Dix

Part 2
1. Basketball (men's); regained the title they had lost in 2004
2. Germany (Matthias Steiner)
3. Rowing (women's coxless pairs)
4. Judo (women's extra-lightweight class)
5. Brazil
6. Leukaemia
7. Wrestling (freestyle, welterweight division)
8. James DeGale (middleweight division)
9. USA (110 to China's 100)
10. Jimmy Page

London 2012

Part 1 – The Build-up
1. Paris
2. Singapore
3. Baseball, softball
4. Boxing
5. Hugh Robertson
6. Keri-Anne Payne (10km open water)
7. Hope Powell
8. Ben Ainslie (sailing)
9. *Survival*
10. G4S

Part 2 – The Games
1. Cardiff (Millennium Stadium). (GB won 1–0)
2. Danny Boyle
3. Seven
4. Handball (also hosted fencing event in modern pentathlon)
5. Eton Dorney (Dorney Lake)
6. David Rudisha (Kenya)
7. Mo Farah (GBR)
8. Six (4 gold, 2 silver)
9. Nicola Adams (flyweight)
10. Games Makers

2. Summer Olympic Sports

Archery
1. Recurve
2. Gold
3. Belgium
4. Dod (Willy, gold, York round; Charlotte ('Lottie') silver, women's double national round)
5. John Williams
6. Darrell Pace (USA)
7. Great Britain
8. Sung-Hyun Park
9. Lord's Cricket Ground
10. Italy
11. Ki Bo-Bae (women's individual/team)
12. China (1992, 2000–2008)

Athletics
Part 1 – Men's track events
1. Alfred Tysoe (800m, 5000m team)
2. Hannes Kolehmainen
3. Guy Butler
4. Jamaica
5. Armin Hary
6. 3000m steeplechase
7. 10000m
8. Frankie Fredericks (Namibia)
9. Mark Lewis-Francis
10. Rashid Ramzi
11. Bahamas (men's 4x400m)
12. Félix Sánchez (Dominican Republic)

Athletics

Part 2 – Women's track events
1. Kinue Hitomi (who died of TB in 1931, aged 24)
2. Betty Cuthbert (100m, 200m, 4x100m, 1956; 400m, 1964)
3. Madeline Manning (USA), 800m; Rosemary Stirling (2:00.15)
4. Irena Szewinska (Poland)
5. Morocco (Nawal El Moutawakel)
6. Wang Junxia
7. Derartu Tulu (Ethiopia)
8. Bahamas
9. 100m
10. Allyson Felix
11. Turkey (1st Asli Çakir Alptekin, 2nd Gamze Bulut)
12. Sally Pearson (12.35 secs)

Part 3 – Men's field events
1. Discus
2. The 'Vaulting Vicar'
3. Parry O'Brien (O'Brien Glide/Style)
4. Triple jump
5. Hammer (1976–88)
6. Adam Nelson
7. Long jump
8. Lithuania
9. Andreas Thorkildsen
10. Tomasz Majewski (shot put)
11. Trinidad and Tobago
12. Greg Rutherford (Lynn Davies won in 1964)

Athletics

Part 4 – Women's field events
1. High jump (1936–1960)
2. Aleksandra Chudina (Long jump/javelin silver, HJ bronze)
3. Discus
4. Ulrike Meyfarth
5. Fatima Whitbread (1984 bronze, 1988 silver)
6. Triple jump
7. Stacey Dragila
8. Hammer
9. Tatyana Lebedeva
10. Belgium
11. Valerie Adams
12. Discus

Part 5 – Marathons, walks and combined events (men)
1. Argentina (Juan Carlos Zabala, Delfo Cabrera)
2. 50km walk
3. UCLA
4. Frank Shorter (USA)
5. East Germany
6. Ecuador
7. Estonia
8. Jon Brown
9. Robert Korzeniowski
10. Decathlon
11. Guatemala
12. Uganda (first was John-Akii Bua, 400m hurdles, 1972)

Athletics

Part 6 – Marathons, walks and combined events (women)
1. Mary Rand (2nd), Mary Peters (4th)
2. 200 metres
3. East Germany
4. Grete Waitz
5. Jackie Joyner-Kersee (WR of 7291 points in 1988)
6. 10km walk
7. Japan (Naoko Takahashi, 2000; Mizuki Noguchi, 2004)
8. Kelly Sotherton
9. Lyudmila Blonska (Ukraine)
10. 20km walk (1:25:02)
11. Ethiopia (2:23:07)
12. Lilli Schwarzkopf

Badminton
1. Indonesia
2. Danish (Poul-Erik Hoyer-Larsen, gold in the men's singles)
3. Ye Zhaoying
4. Netherlands
5. Simon Archer
6. Taufik Hidayat
7. Nathan Robertson and Gail Emms
8. Zhang Ning
9. Lin Dan
10. Indonesia
11. Denmark (1 silver, 1 bronze)
12. India

Basketball

Part 1 (1936–1980)
1. Canada
2. James Naismith
3. First African-American to represent the USA in basketball
4. Iraq
5. Uruguay
6. Boston Celtics
7. Brazil
8. Yugoslavia
9. Sasha Belov (USSR)
10. Soviet Union (1976–1980)
11. Bulgaria
12. Italy

Part 2 (1984–2012)
1. Michael Jordan
2. Teresa Edwards
3. Harlem Globetrotters
4. Brazil
5. Charles Barkley (18 points)
6. David Robinson
7. Lisa Leslie
8. Lithuania (85–83)
9. Puerto Rico (92–73)
10. Australia
11. Kevin Durant
12. France

Boxing

Part 1 (1904–1980)
1. He won gold in two weight categories at the same Olympics (bantamweight, featherweight).
2. Featherweight
3. Heavyweight
4. Harry Mallin
5. Argentina (Carmelo Robeldo, 1932; Oscar Casanovas, 1936)
6. Val Barker Trophy
7. Light-welterweight, light-middleweight
8. Flyweight (–51 kg)
9. Chris Finnegan
10. George Foreman (1968)
11. György Gedó (1968–80)
12. Michael Spinks (USA)

Part 2 (1984–2012)
1. Evander Holyfield (lost to New Zealand's Kevin Barry)
2. Canada (super heavyweight)
3. Oscar de la Hoya (USA)
4. Vladimir Klitschko (Ukraine)
5. Félix Savón
6. Featherweight
7. Mario Kindelán
8. Frankie Gavin (lightweight)
9. Katie Taylor
10. Luke Campbell
11. Middleweight
12. Kazakhstan (Serik Sapiyev)

Canoeing

1. 200 metres
2. Repechage
3. Canadian pairs, 1000m
4. Denmark
5. Gert Fredriksson
6. East Germany
7. New Zealand
8. Hungary
9. Slovakia
10. Tim Brabants
11. Ed McKeever
12. Men's C-1 (Canadian singles)

Cycling

Part 1 (1896–1988)

1. France
2. Italy
3. Reg Harris
4. Belgium (1st André Noyelle, 2nd Robert Grondelaers)
5. Sante Gaiadorni
6. Eddy Merckx
7. Daniel Morelon
8. West Germany
9. Road race (79.2 km)
10. USA
11. Denmark
12. 1970s (1976)

Cycling

Part 2 (1992–2012)
1. Chris Boardman
2. Miguel Indurain (Spain)
3. Paola Pezzo
4. Jan Ullrich (won the Tour in 1997)
5. Leontine van Moorsel
6. 1km time trial
7. Shanaze Reade
8. Wendy Houvenaghel
9. Chris Froome
10. Omnium
11. Hadleigh Farm
12. Maris Strombergs

Diving
1. 1900s (1904)
2. Twelve
3. USA
4. Pat McCormick
5. Klaus Dibiasi
6. Greg Louganis (3m springboard, 10m platform)
7. 13
8. Australia
9. Canada
10. Matthew Mitcham
11. Wu Minxia (partnered in London by He Zi)
12. David Boudia (10m platform gold/synchronised bronze)

Equestrian

Part 1 (1900–1976)
1. Belgium
2. Netherlands
3. Team eventing (bronze)
4. Sweden (Gelling Persson ineligible as he was a sergeant)
5. Pat Smythe (on *Flanagan*)
6. Raimundo D'Inzeo (on *Posillipo*)
7. Argentina (silver in individual eventing for Carlos Moratorio)
8. Jane Bullen (on *Our Nobby*)
9. *Cornishman V.* Films were *Dead Cert* (1974) and *International Velvet* (1978)
10. Liselott Linsenhoff (on *Piaff*)
11. Alwin Schockemoehle (on *Warwick Rex*)
12. *Goodwill*

Part 2 (1980–2012)
1. Soviet Union
2. Mark Todd (on *Charisma*)
3. Reine Klimke
4. *Gigolo*
5. New Zealand (1st Blyth Tait on *Reddy Teddy*, 2nd Sally Clark on *Squirrel Hill*)
6. Andrew Hoy (on *Darien Powers*)
7. Bettina Hoy (on *Ringwood Cockatoo*)
8. Theodora ('Anky') van Grunsven (on *Salinero*)
9. Tina Cook (individual/team eventing), on *Miners Frolic*
10. Michael Jung (on *Sam*)
11. Nick Skelton (on *Big Star*)
12. *Valegro*

Fencing
1. Three, each of three minutes (if 15 hits have not been scored)
2. *Barrage*
3. Nedo Nadi (individual foil/sabre; team épée/foil/sabre)
4. Denmark
5. Hungary
6. Christian d'Oriola
7. Soviet Union
8. France
9. USA (Albertson Van Zo Post won two golds in 1904)
10. Valentina Vezzali
11. Britta Heidemann
12. Venezuela

Football

Part 1 (1900–1968)
1. Three
2. Upton Park FC
3. Netherlands
4. Egypt
5. Poland
6. AC Milan (Gunnar Gren, Gunnar Nordahl, Nils Liedholm)
7. Soviet Union
8. Ferenc Puskás (Hungary 2–0 Yugoslavia)
9. India
10. Yugoslavia
11. Japan
12. Four (3 from Bulgaria, 1 from Hungary)

Football

Part 2 (1972–2012)
1. Kazimierz Deyna
2. Dunga
3. Zambia
4. Kiko (Spain 3–2 Poland)
5. China
6. Cameroon (won 5–3 on pens after a 2–2 draw)
7. Carlos Tévez (Argentina)
8. Mariel ('Mia') Hamm
9. Brazil
10. Daniel Sturridge
11. Canada (beat GB 2–0; lost 3–4 to the USA)
12. Oribe Peralta (Mexico 2–1 Brazil)

Gymnastics
Part 1 – Men's events
1. 1890s (1896)
2. Germany (parallel bars, 1896)
3. Men's all-around championship
4. Leon Štukelj
5. Viktor Chukarin (USSR)
6. Japan
7. Sawao Kato
8. Alexander Dityatin (USSR)
9. Vitaly Scherbo (Unified Team)
10. Zou Kai (floor, high bar, team)
11. Kōhei Uchimura (also silvers in team event, floor exercise)
12. Pommel horse (Louis Smith, silver; Max Whitlock, bronze)

Gymnastics

Part 2 – Women's events
1. 1920s (1928; in the team all-around event)
2. Czechoslovakia
3. Maria Gorokhovskaya (2 gold, 5 silver)
4. Hungary
5. Věra Čáslavská
6. Nellie Kim
7. Ecaterina Szabo
8. Balance beam
9. Romania
10. Russia
11. Gabby Douglas
12. Uneven bars

Handball
1. Austria
2. Yugoslavia
3. 1970s (1976)
4. USSR (1976–80)
5. Kuwait
6. Andrei Lavrov (USSR, 1988; Unified Team, '92; Russia, 2000)
7. South Korea
8. Denmark
9. Iceland (lost 23–28)
10. Basketball Arena (earlier rounds held in the Copper Box)
11. Sweden (22–21)
12. Montenegro (lost 23–26)

Hockey

1. Great Britain (1908, 1920)
2. India (won 30 consecutive matches)
3. West Germany
4. Pakistan
5. Zimbabwe
6. Ian Taylor
7. Imran Sherwani
8. South Korea (5th in 1996, 2nd in 2000)
9. Argentina (women's tournament, silver)
10. Australia
11. New Zealand (3–1)
12. Germany

Judo

1. Japanese (Takejhide Nakatani, lightweight division, 1964)
2. Netherlands (Antonius Geesnik, 1964; Willem Ruska, 1972)
3. Golden score period (of 3 mins)
4. Neil Adams (silvers at -71 kg in 1984, -78 kg in 1988)
5. Middleweight
6. Kate Howey (middleweight bronze, 1992; -70 kg silver, 2000)
7. Tadahiro Nomura
8. Mongolia
9. China
10. Half middleweight (-81 kg)
11. Teddy Riner
12. Gemma Gibbons

Modern Pentathlon

1. 200m
2. Sweden
3. Lars Hall (Sweden)
4. Hungary
5. Jim Fox
6. Pavel Lednev
7. Poland
8. Russia (Dmitri Svatkowksi, 2000; Andrei Moiseyev, 2004–8)
9. Swimming
10. Running and shooting
11. David Svoboda
12. Great Britain

Rowing

Part 1 (1900–1976)

1. Germany
2. The Seine (Paris)
3. Jack Beresford (3 gold, 2 silver)
4. USA
5. Trinity College
6. Hugh 'Jumbo' Edwards (coxless pairs, coxless fours)
7. Richard Burnell (double sculls; with Bert Bushnell). His father Charles had won gold in the eights in 1908.
8. Argentina (men's double sculls)
9. Vyacheslav Ivanov
10. New Zealand
11. 1000 metres
12. Norway

Rowing

Part 2 (1980–2012)
1. East Germany
2. Perti Karpinnen
3. 2000 metres
4. Australia
5. Germany
6. Elisabeta Lipa (won eight medals inc five gold, 1984–2004)
7. New Zealand
8. Romania
9. Zac Purchase
10. Coxless four
11. Katherine Grainger (won double sculls with Anna Watkins)
12. USA

Sailing

Part 1 (1900–1984)
1. Handicap races, separate finals (two or three)
2. Wright (Cyril and Dorothy)
3. Kiel
4. Paul Elvstrøm (Finn class)
5. Swallow
6. New Zealand
7. Bahamas (Durward Knowles, C Cecil Cooke)
8. Rodney Pattisson (Flying Dutchman class)
9. Lake Ontario
10. Finland
11. USA
12. Russell Coutts

Sailing

Part 2 (1984–2012)
1. East Germany (International Soling)
2. Europe, Sailboard
3. Spanish
4. Laser
5. Robert Scheidt
6. Yngling
7. Iain Percy, Andrew Simpson
8. Paul Goodison
9. Dorset (Weymouth and Portland National Sailing Academy)
10. 49er
11. Elliott 6m
12. Australia (3 golds, 1 silver)

Shooting
1. 1890s (1896)
2. USA
3. Bisley Camp (Surrey)
4. Bob Braithwaite (clay pigeon event)
5. Canada
6. Malcolm Cooper
7. Richard Faulds
8. Skeet
9. Matthew Emmons
10. Katerina Emmons
11. Double trap
12. South Korea (3 golds, 2 silver)

Swimming

Part 1 – Men's events
1. Hungary (1896, 1900)
2. Henry Taylor
3. Japan
4. Murray Rose
5. Don Schollander
6. Swedish (Gunnar Larsson)
7. Valdimir Salnikov
8. Matt Biondi
9. Alexander Popov
10. Japanese (Kosuke Kitajima)
11. 100m butterfly, 200m medley
12. Sun Yang

Part 2 – Women's events
1. Sarah ('Fanny') Durack
2. Judy Grinham
3. Dawn Fraser
4. Shirley Babashoff
5. 100m freestyle (both timed at 55.92 secs)
6. Kristin Otto
7. Michelle Smith (but allowed to keep her medals)
8. Inge de Bruijn
9. 800m freestyle (8 mins 14.10 secs)
10. 10km marathon
11. Missy Franklin
12. Ye Shiwen

Synchronised Swimming
1. 1980s (1984)
2. Canada
3. Josephson (Sarah and Karen)
4. USA
5. France (vetoed by the Minister of Youth and Sport, Guy Drut)
6. They achieved the first perfect 10 score (artistic impression)
7. Japan
8. *Pirates of the Caribbean*
9. Egypt
10. Spain
11. The Aquatics Centre
12. 12

Table Tennis
1. 1980s (1988)
2. Top 28 (each nation limited to two players)
3. Yugoslavia
4. South Korea
5. Sweden (Jan-Ove Waldner)
6. Deng Yaping
7. France
8. Hong Kong
9. Germany (silver, men's team event)
10. Natalia Partyka
11. ExCeL London (The ExCeL Exhibition Centre)
12. Singapore (women's singles/team)

Taekwondo

1. 1980s (1988)
2. Four (fly/feather/welter/heavyweight)
3. Two
4. Vietnam
5. Steven Lopez
6. +67 kg
7. Iran
8. South Korea
9. Afghanistan (he also won 68 kg bronze in 2012)
10. Jade Jones
11. Lutalo Muhammad
12. Gabon

Tennis

Part 1 – Men's events

1. Max Decugis
2. Henri Cochet (men's singles, men's doubles)
3. Miloslav Mečíř (Czechoslovakia)
4. Jim Courier (USA)
5. Sergi Bruguera
6. Canada (Sebastian Lareau & Daniel Nestor)
7. Nicolas Massu of Chile (men's singles, men's doubles)
8. Andy Murray (GBR)
9. Fernando González (Chile)
10. Juan Martín del Potro (ARG). Match lasted 4 hours 26 mins.
11. Novak Djokovic (SRB)
12. France (Michaël Llodra & Jo Wilfried Tsonga)

Tennis

Part 2 – Women's events
1. Dorothea ('Dolly') Lambert Chambers (GBR)
2. Kitty Godfree (née McCane)
3. Helen Wills Moody
4. Steffi Graf (West Germany)
5. Gigi Fernandez & Mary Jo Fernandez (USA)
6. Arancha Sanchez Vicario (Spain)
7. China (Li Ting, Sun Tiantian)
8. Venus Williams (women's singles, women's doubles)
9. Dinara Safina
10. Jelena Jankovic (Serbia)
11. Maria Sharapova (RUS)
12. Belarus (Victoria Azarenka & Max Mirnyi)

Triathlon
1. 1500m
2. 10km
3. Olivier Marceau
4. Canada
5. New Zealand (Hamish Carter gold, Bevan Doherty silver)
6. Michelle Dillon
7. Alistair Brownlee (won 2009 & 2011 triathlon world titles)
8. Germany
9. Australia (Emma Snowsill gold, Emma Moffat bronze)
10. The Serpentine
11. Switzerland (Nicola Spirig, 1st), Sweden (Lisa Nordén, 2nd)
12. Spain (Javier Gómez)

Volleyball
1. 15 (first four sets played to 25 points)
2. *Libero*
3. Poland
4. Yugoslavia
5. Japan (at the 1964 Tokyo Games)
6. Peru
7. Cuba
8. Bondi Beach
9. Brazil
10. Horse Guards Parade
11. USA
12. Russia (beat Brazil in five sets)

Water Polo
1. 1900s (1900)
2. Great Britain (1900–1920)
3. Yugoslavia
4. Goal difference
5. Spain (9–8)
6. Slovakia
7. Australia
8. Hungary
9. Netherlands
10. Croatia
11. USA
12. Eight

Weightlifting
1. 75 kg
2. Denmark
3. USA
4. Vassily Alekseyev
5. Bulgaria
6. Light heavyweight
7. Naim Süleymanoğlu
8. Super-heavyweight
9. Russia
10. London ExCeL (The ExCeL Exhibition Centre)
11. Zoe Smith (GB record with clean and jerk lift of 121 kg)
12. Kazakhstan

Wrestling
1. Three
2. Soviet Union (62: Freestyle 34, Greco-Roman 28)
3. Great Britain (last medal was in 1908)
4. Sweden (1920–1932)
5. France
6. Beloglazov (Anatoly, flyweight; Sergei, bantamweight)
7. 48 kg
8. Canada (Carol Huynh; flyweight, 48 kg)
9. Ara Abrahamian
10. Cuba
11. Artur Taymazov
12. Russia (Natalia Vorobieva, 72 kg)

Discontinued Sports
1. Croquet
2. Cricket (Devon and Somerset Wanderers Cricket Club)
3. Lacrosse
4. *Jeu de Paume* (or real tennis)
5. Tug of war
6. Pelota (demonstration sport in 1924, 1968 and 1992)
7. Rugby (Australia, 1912; USA, 1920)
8. Cuba (1992–1996, 2004)
9. South Korea
10. Japan
11. USA (1996–2004)
12. Polo

3. Summer Olympics Numbers

Part 1 – A Question of Age
1. (a) 10 (10 yr 218 days); bronze in men's team parallel bars
2. (b) 53 (53 yr 275 days); won women's double national round
3. (b) 61 (61 yr 4 days); won free rifle – 1000 yards event
4. (d) 17 (17 yr 226 days); gold in 4x100m freestyle relay
5. (d) 72 (72 yr 280 days); team 100m running deer, double shots
6. (c) 14 (14 yr 309 days); won 1500m freestyle
7. (c) 13 (13 yr 267 days)
8. (c) 48 (48 yr 115 days)
9. (d) 70 (70 yr 5 days)
10. (d) 71 (71 yr 127 days)
11. (c) 7
12. (b) 17–34

Part 2 – How many?
1. (a) 14
2. (b) 9
3. (c) 56
4. (d) 42 (his father had eight wives)
5. (d) 80
6 (c) 5
7. (a) 16
8. (c) 204
9. (a) 26
10. (c) 541
11. (b) 32
12. (b) 104

Part 3 – Name the Year

1. (d) 393 AD
2. (c) 1996 (10327 competitors in Atlanta)
3. (d) 1972 (1095 women competed in Munich)
4. (b) 1964
5. (c) 1952
6. (b) 1984 (individual road race)
7. (a) 1900 (four events)
8. (c) 1912
9. (d) 1992
10. (a) 1980 (Kenya boycotted those Games; Poland's Bronisław Malinowski won gold)
11. (d) 2000
12. (b) 2005 (6 July)

Part 4 – Placings and scores

1. (b) 6th (Priscilla Welch, 1984; Mara Yamauchi, 2008)
2. (a) 3rd (Malcolm Nokes, 1924)
3. (a) 19–8 (in an outdoor match affected by rain)
4. (b) 6th
5. (a) 3rd
6. (c) 3–1
7. (d) 3–2
8. (b) 2–1
9. (d) 9–2
10. (a) 10th
11. (d) 44–15
12. (b) 30th (Lee Merrien)

Part 5 – A Matter of Time
1. (d) 11 hrs 40 mins
2. (c) 10.3
3. (a) 3.35.6
4. (d) 4 mins 8 secs (2:12.11.2 to the runner-up's 2:16.19.2)
5. (b) 14:58.27
6. (a) 0.80
7. (b) 12.91
8. (c) 19.30
9. (d) 18 (50:39.54 to the runner-up's 50:21.54)
10. (c) 40.82
11. (b) 1:40.91
12. (a) 29:07

Part 6 – Weights and Measures
1. (d) 8.90m
2. (c) 18.09m
3. (a) 1.50m (4ft 11in)
4. (c) 167 kg (25stone 8lbs)
5. (a) 5.05m
6. (c) 2.29m (7ft 6in)
7. (b) 56 kg
8. (d) 78.18m
9. (c) 69-75 kg
10. (a) 1.45 (4ft 9in)
11. (c) 375–400g
12. (d) 218 kg (34st 5lbs)

4. Summer Olympics Mixed Bag

First Things First

Part 1 (1896–1976)
1. 100 metres
2. 1500m
3. Long jump
4. Canoeing
5. Discus
6. Anita Lonsbrough (who won Olympic 200m breaststroke gold in 1960, SPOTY in 1962 and carried the flag in 1964)
7. Boxing (light welterweight)
8. Alcohol (Hans-Gunnar Liljenwall was the offender)
9. Nadia Comăneci (Romania)
10. Wyomia Tyus (USA), who won 100m gold in 1964 and 1968.

Part 2 (1980–2008)
1. Ronald Reagan (Los Angeles 1984)
2. Archery (she placed 35th in the women's individual event)
3. Sweden
4. Suriname (He won the 100m butterfly)
5. Namibia (Frankie Fredericks won 100 and 200m silvers)
6. Israel
7. Women's 1500m (she placed 8th)
8. Wrestling (freestyle)
9. India
10. Panama

First Things First

Part 3 – London 2012
1. Shooting (women's 10m air rifle)
2. Lizzie Armitstead (women's individual road race)
3. Oscar Pistorious (South Africa)
4. Judo (+78 kg division)
5. Kirani James
6. Beach volleyball
7. Botswana
8. Cyprus
9. Lithuania
10. Ian Millar (first competed at the Olympics in 1972)

Controversy

Part 1 (1908–1980)
1. The 400 metres (Disqualification of John Carpenter (USA) in the original race and his banning from the re-run led both two team-mates in the final to boycott the re-run in support of him)
2. Paavo Nurmi (Finland)
3. Cycling (1000m sprint)
4. Czechoslovakia (where the Communist Party had taken power)
5. Soviet Union and Hungary
6. Dawn Fraser
7. Tommie Smith, John Carlos
8. USA and USSR
9. Boris Onischenko
10. Pole vault

Controversy

Part 2 (1984–2012)
1. 3000m
2. Daley Thompson (referring allegedly to Carl Lewis)
3. Roy Jones Jr
4. USA (lost to Japan; a committee reversed the original result)
5. Marion Jones (USA)
6. Kostas Kenteris, Ekaterina Thanou
7. Blake Aldridge
8. Taekwondo
9. North Korea (South Korea flag shown by mistake)
10. Badminton (Four women's doubles pairs were expelled for attempting to throw a group match in order to secure a better draw in the next round.)

Family Ties

Part 1 (1900–1960s)
1. Tennis (men's doubles)
2. Sailing (6 metre class)
3. Rowing: Jack Kelly (1920s), 'Ran' Laurie (1948)
4. Charlotte Rampling (Her father Godfrey Rampling won gold at 4x400m in 1936 and died aged 100 in 2009.)
5. Father and son
6. Bobby Davro
7. Football
8. Javelin
9. Press (Irina and Tamara)
10. Violet Webb and Janet Simpson. (Vi Webb (later Simpson) won 4x100m bronze at the 1932 Los Angeles Games and daughter Janet also won bronze in the same event in 1964.)

Family Ties

Part 2 (1968–2012)
1. Equestrian
2. Rowing (coxless pairs)
3. Hammer
4. Joyner (Al won triple jump gold, Jackie long jump silver)
5. Searle (Greg and Jonny). Greg won bronze in the eights, 2012
6. Synchronised swimming (duet)
7. Iran (1948–52)
8. Ernest Hemingway (Great nephew Matt Hemingway won silver in the high jump)
9. Slovakia
10. Chambers (Richard and Peter)

Find the Lady
1. Gertrude Ederle (USA)
2. Olga Fikotová
3. Sofia of Spain
4. Christine von Saltza
5. Ludmila Tourischeva
6. Joan Benoit
7. Gail Devers
8. Stephanie Cook
9. Joanne Jackson
10. Meseret Defar

Great Britain at the Olympics

Part 1 (1896–1976)
1. Weightlifting (one-handed lift)
2. Charlotte ('Chattie') Cooper
3. Rugby (union)
4. Water polo
5. Swimming (200m breaststroke)
6. Lord Burghley (400m hurdles)
7. Fencing (silver in team épée, 1960; individual épée, 1964)
8. Rowing (as coxswain in the coxed pairs event)
9. David Broome
10. 200m, 4x100m

Part 2 (1976–2008)
1. Brendan Foster (10000m bronze)
2. 100m hurdles
3. Andy Holmes
4. Archery (individual, team)
5. 200m
6. Pippa Funnell (individual eventing)
7. Sailing (470 class)
8. Mark Foster
9. Nicole Cooke (individual road race)
10. Louis Smith

Great Britain at the Olympics

Part 3 – London 2012
1. Helen Glover and Heather Stanning (women's pair event)
2. Laura Trott (cycling), Charlotte Dujardin (equestrian)
3. Michael Jamieson (200m breaststroke). (Dániel Gyurta won in WR of 2:07.28)
4. Pete Waterfield
5. Hockey
6. Alan Campbell
7. 100m hurdles (12.54 secs; world best in a heptathlon)
8. Canoeing (C-2 team)
9. Equestrian (individual dressage)
10. Samantha Murray

Memorable Moments
1. Ann Packer
2. Gymnastics (all-around team event)
3. He stopped to rescue two capsized competitors
4. Derek Redmond (400m semi-final)
5. Muhammad Ali
6. Equatorial Guinea
7. Men's marathon (Cornelius Horan was the 'priest'. The runner, Brazil's Vanderlei de Lima, recovered to take bronze. He later received the Pierre de Coubertin medal for sportsmanship.)
8. Georgia and Russia (Nina Salukvadze, gold; Natalia Paderina, silver)
9. Rowing (men's single sculls, repechage)
10. Men's 4x400m (semi-final)

Multi-talented Olympians

Part 1 – Other sports
1. Tennis (men's doubles)
2. Weightlifting
3. Cricket
4. Max Woosnam
5. Mildred 'Babe' Didriksen (USA)
6. Bob Hayes (won 100m and 4x100m golds in 1964 and the Super Bowl with Dallas Cowboys in the 1971 season)
7. Swimming (4x100m freestyle relay, silver)
8. Cycling
9. Rebecca Romero
10. Modern pentathlon (she finished 19th)

Part 2 – Other fields
1. George S Patton
2. Rowing (eight-oared shell with coxswain)
3. New Zealand (1967–72)
4. (Clarence Linden) 'Buster' Crabbe
5. Sir Peter Scott (O-Jolle class)
6. *Goldfinger* (as 'Oddjob')
7. Micheline Ostermeyer (shot put, discus)
8. The World Bank Group (1995–2005)
9. Sir Menzies ('Ming') Campbell (ex-leader of the Lib Dems)
10. Bob Seagren (1968 pole vault champion)

Summer Olympics Legends

Part 1 (1920–1976)
1. Nine (in the period 1920–1928)
2. Long jump
3. 80m hurdles
4. Four (5000m gold, 1948; 5000m, 10000m, Mar gold, 1952)
5. Larissa Latynina
6. Abebe Bikila (Ethiopia)
7. Al Oerter (discus)
8. Olga Korbut
9. Nine (two in 1968, seven in 1972)
10. Lasse Viren (Finland)

Part 2 (1980–2012)
1. Gymnastics
2. Four (1500m gold, 1980–84; 800m silver, 1980–84)
3. Long jump
4. Austria
5. Michael Johnson (USA)
6. Ian Thorpe
7. 22 (18 gold, 2 silver, 2 bronze)
8. Keirin
9. Ben Ainslie (GBR)
10. 9.63 secs

The Summer Olympics at the Movies

1. Leni Riefenstahl
2. Charlie Chan (*Charlie Chan at the Olympics*)
3. Burt Lancaster
4. Kon Ichikawa
5. Michael Winner
6. Colin Welland
7. Munich 1972
8. *Letters from Iwo Jima*
9. *Salute*
10. *Fast Girls*

The Summer Olympics and Music

1. Richard Strauss
2. John Williams
3. *One Moment in Time*
4. José Carreras
5. Gladys Knight
6. *Unity*
7. Leona Lewis
8. Stereophonics
9. Emile Sandé
10. George Michael

The One and Only

Part 1 – General
1. Ray Ewry of the USA (standing jumps events, 1900–1908)
2. Fencing (women's individual foil, 1956)
3. 10000m (1964)
4. Javelin (1952)
5. Dorothy Odam/Tyler, won high jump silver in 1936 and 1948
6. Marc Rosset (men's singles, 1992)
7. Hungarian (He won six team golds in the period 1932–60)
8. Steve Backley (javelin, 1992–2000)
9. Canoeing (Eight golds in total, 1980–2004)
10. Great Britain

Part 2 (1908–2012)
1. River Clyde (12m class)
2. A Nobel Prize. (Awarded the 1959 Nobel Peace Prize for his efforts to secure an international treaty on arms control.)
3. The Victoria Cross
4. Boxing (light heavyweight)
5. Mexico
6. Cycling
7. (Wheelchair) Fencing
8. Syria
9. Mark Cavendish
10. Tunisia

Quote...Unquote
1. US athlete Jesse Owens (won four Olympic golds in 1936 but was ignored by US president Franklin D Roosevelt)
2. Bob Mathias (aged 17 when he won the decathlon)
3. John Sherwood
4. Teofilio Stevenson
5. Steve Ovett (who would finish third)
6. Barry Davies
7. Michael Johnson (USA)
8. Gary Hill Jr
9. Bert le Clos (father of Chad le Clos, winner of 200m butterfly)
10. Ben Ainslie (Finn class, sailing)

The USA at the Summer Olympics

Part 1 (1900–1952)
1. Golf (women's tournament)
2. Archie Hahn
3. Rugby (union)
4. Diving
5. Major-General Douglas MacArthur
6. Jean Shiley (both women cleared 1.657m)
7. Eleanor Holm
8. 200m
9. Sailing (6m team yachting)
10. The FBI

The USA at the Summer Olympics

Part 2 (1960–2012)
1. Ralph Boston (gold 1960, silver 1964, bronze 1968)
2. Basketball
3. Steve Prefontaine (4th in the 5000m)
4. John Naber
5. Sailing (Star class)
6. Janet Evans
7. Bill Clinton (Atlanta 1996)
8. Softball
9. Justin Gatlin (100m bronze, 4x100m silver)
10. Shooting (women's skeet)

Trivia Teasers

Part 1 (1904–1956)
1. He had a wooden leg
2. Bicycle polo
3. Alexandria (Egypt)
4. Surfing
5. Norway (Crown Prince Olav; later reigned as Olav V)
6. 400m hurdles (Won by the Irish athlete Bob Tisdall who knocked a hurdle down, an error which in that era disqualified a performance for world record consideration, so the runner-up, Glenn Hardin (USA), was instead credited with the record)
7. Adolf Hitler (fondled Helen Stephens, the 100m champion)
8. Athletics (100m, 200m)
9. Wrestling
10. Lorraine Crapp

Trivia Teasers

Part 2 (1960–2008)
1. The Pope (John XXIII), from his palace at Castel Gondolfo
2. Mary Rand (1964, long jump)
3. Lee Evans (400m)
4. Geoff Capes (shot put)
5. Dame Mary Glen-Haig (IOC member from 1982–1990)
6. Albania (boycotted all Summer Games from 1976–1988)
7. Martin Luther King
8. Handball
9. Togo (he won bronze in men's slalom K-1 event)
10. Barcelona 1992

Part 3 (London 2012/general)
1. Hugh Bonneville
2. Weightlifting (men's 105 kg)
3. He ran an escort agency (legal in New Zealand since 2003)
4. Shooting (10 metre air rifle event)
5. Theodore Roosevelt (1901–09)
6. Kim Collins (St Kitts & Nevis)
7. Football (she punched US player Abby Wambach in the face)
8. Bangladesh (world's 9th most populous country, 142 million)
9. Detroit
10. Hungary (475)

Last but not Least

Part 1 – General
1. Golf
2. Richard Meade (1972, equestrian individual eventing)
3. Unified Team (1992)
4. Tyrell Biggs (1984)
5. Spain (1992)
6. 10km track walk
7. Pakistan
8. Andre Agassi (1996)
9. South Korea (Ryu Seung-Min, men's singles, 2004)
10. Lithuania

Part 2 – Great Britain
1. Daley Thompson (decathlon, 1984)
2. 1988 (men's event)
3. Adrian Moorhouse (1988, 100m breaststroke)
4. Water polo
5. Equestrian (individual eventing, 2004)
6. Eric Liddell (1924)
7. 1960 (men's)
8. 1980 (0 golds, 1 silver, 2 bronze)
9. Henry Taylor (swimming, 1908)
10. Anthony Joshua (super heavyweight)

10. WINTER OLYMPICS ANSWERS

5. Winter Olympic History

Overview
1. Chamonix
2. Curling
3. Adolf Hitler
4. St Moritz
5. Sapporo (Japan), in 1972
6. Innsbruck (Austria)
7. Sarajevo (then in Yugoslavia, now in Bosnia-Herzegovina)
8. Rhona Martin
9. Amy Williams
10. Sochi

Chamonix 1924
1. International Winter Sports Week
2. Speed skating (500m)
3. Figure skating, ice hockey
4. Finnish
5. Cross-country (Nordic) skiing
6. Switzerland
7. Military patrol
8. Canada
9. Figure skating (Ladies' singles)
10. Norway (4 golds and 17 medals in total)

St Moritz 1928

1. Japan
2. Mexico
3. Cresta Run
4. Five
5. Speed skating (10000m)
6. Sonja Henje
7. Sweden
8. Cross-country skiing (18km), Nordic combined (individual)
9. Skeleton (men's singles event)
10. USA

Lake Placid 1932

1. Franklin D Roosevelt (then Governor of New York state)
2. Great Britain's
3. Speed skating
4. Bobsleigh (four-man)
5. Germany
6. 5000m, 10000m
7. Austria
8. 50km
9. Norway
10. Dog sled racing

Garmisch-Partenkirchen 1936

1. Alpine skiing
2. Bulgaria
3. Speed skating (golds at 500m, 5000m, 10000m)
4. Switzerland
5. Ice hockey
6. Figure skating (women's singles)
7. 40km (4x10km)
8. Ski jumping
9. Germany (Franz Pfnür, Christl Cranz)
10. Norway

St Moritz 1948

1. Germany, Japan (because of their role in World War II)
2. Chile
3. Winter pentathlon
4. Czechoslovakia
5. Double Axel
6. Henri Orellier
7. Austria
8. Switzerland
9. Nino Bibbia
10. Norway, Sweden

Oslo 1952
1. King George VI (Great Britain)
2. New Zealand
3. Speed skating (1500m, 5000m, 10000m)
4. Jeannette Altwegg
5. Alpine skiing (slalom, giant slalom)
6. Cross-country skiing
7. Norway
8. Germany (Paul and Ria Falk)
9. Bandy
10. 10000 metres

Cortina D'Ampezzo 1956
1. 1944 (cancelled because of WWII)
2. Figure skating
3. Soviet Union (16 including 7 gold)
4. Toni Sailer (downhill, slalom, giant slalom)
5. Finland (Antti Hyvärinen, Aulis Kallakorpi)
6. Speed skating (500m, 1500m)
7. Slalom
8. Sweden
9. Hungary (Mariana and László Nagy)
10. Soviet Union

Squaw Valley 1960
1. Richard Nixon
2. Biathlon
3. Bobsleigh
4. Speed skating (four events)
5. Germany (Helmut Recknagel)
6. Canada
7. Alpine skiing (silvers in downhill and giant slalom)
8. Cross-country skiing
9. USA
10. Figure skating

Innsbruck 1964
1. India, Mongolia
2. The use of computers
3. Luge
4. Speed skating
5. France
6. Figure skating (ladies' singles)
7. Soviet Union (1st Vladimir Melanin, 2nd Aleksandr Privalov)
8. Canada
9. Robin Dixon and Tony Nash
10. Austria (4 golds and 12 medals in total)

Grenoble 1968

1. Charles de Gaulle, President of France
2. Drugs, gender
3. Morocco
4. Jean-Claude Killy
5. Bobsleigh (two-man, four-man)
6. USA
7. Cross-country skiing
8. Soviet Union (Oleg Protopopov and Ludmila Belousova)
9. Romania (two-man event)
10. Speed skating (500m)

Sapporo 1972

1. Emperor Hirohito
2. Philippines
3. Canada
4. Speed skating
5. Cross-country skiing (5km, 10km, 3x5km)
6. Biathlon (individual 20km event)
7. Japan
8. Swiss
9. Spain (Paquito Fernández)
10. East Germany (4 golds and 14 medals in total)

Innsbruck 1976

1. Denver (withdrew after a plan to finance the Games was rejected in a public vote in Colorado)
2. Andorra, San Marino
3. Speed skating
4. West Germany
5. Franz Klammer (Austria), 102 km/h (63mph)
6. Soviet Union
7. John Curry (men's singles)
8. Dorothy Hamill
9. East Germany
10. Biathlon (20km, 4x7.5km relay)

Lake Placid 1980

1. The People's Republic of China
2. Walter Mondale
3. Eric Heiden
4. Robin Cousins
5. Liechtenstein
6. Ingemar Stenmark
7. Nordic combined (individual)
8. 'The Miracle on Ice'
9. Cross-country skiing (30km, 50km, 4x10km relay)
10. East Germany (23 medals in total)

Sarajevo 1984
1. Juan Antonio Samaranch
2. Egypt
3. Yugoslavia
4. Cross-country skiing (5km, 10km, 20km)
5. Figure skating (ladies' singles)
6. Biathlon
7. Bill Johnson
8. East Germany
9. Canada (1000m, 1500m)
10. Austria

Calgary 1988
1. Queen Elizabeth II
2. Super giant slalom (or Super G)
3. Speed skating
4. Alpine skiing
5. Ski jumping
6. Speed skating
7. Katarina Witt
8. Alberto Tomba (slalom, giant slalom)
9. Biathlon (10km, 20km)
10. Soviet Union (11 golds)

Albertville 1992
1. Francois Mitterand
2. Michel Platini
3. Freestyle skiing, short track speed skating
4. Cross country skiing (4x5km relay)
5. Norway
6. Austria
7. Bonnie Blair (500m, 1000m)
8. Unified Team
9. Switzerland
10. New Zealand

Lillehammer 1994
1. Harald V
2. Ice hockey, figure skating
3. Cross-country skiing
4. Speed skating
5. Canada
6. Switzerland
7. Nancy Kerrigan (USA), ladies' singles event
8. Third
9. Canada
10. Norway (26, including 10 gold). Russia won 23 inc 11 gold.

Nagano 1998
1. Emperor Akihito
2. Snowboarding
3. Ice hockey
4. USA
5. Cross-country skiing
6. Hermann Maier
7. Bulgaria
8. Czech Republic (won 1–0)
9. Alpine skiing (downhill, combined)
10. Australia

Salt Lake City 2002
1. US President George W Bush
2. Jacques Rogge
3. John Williams
4. Hong Kong
5. Biathlon (10km, 12.5km, 20km, 4 x 7.5km relay)
6. Finland
7. China (Yang Yang)
8. Freestyle skiing (aeriels)
9. Canada
10. Germany (36)

Turin 2006
1. Luciano Pavarotti (he died on 6 Sept 2007)
2. Sophia Loren
3. Cross-country skiing
4. Short track speed skating
5. Biathlon
6. Croatia
7. Speed skating (1000m)
8. Canada
9. Sweden
10. Shelley Rudman (silver in skeleton)

Vancouver 2010
1. 'Own the Podium'
2. Georgia
3. Freestyle skiing (men's moguls)
4. Marit Bjørgen
5. Alpine skiing
6. Austria
7. Switzerland
8. Bode Miller
9. Canada
10. Germany

6. Winter Olympic Sports

Alpine Skiing
1. Downhill, Super G
2. German (Christel Cranz, won the combined event in 1936)
3. USA
4. Italy
5. Jean Vuarnet (men's downhill event)
6. Switzerland
7. Annemarie Moser-Pröll (downhill)
8. Lasse Kjus
9. Women's giant slalom
10. Graham Bell (placed 23rd)
11. Norwegian
12. Men's downhill

Biathlon
1. 30 secs
2. 50 metres
3. Five
4. 1960s (1960; men's event only)
5. Sweden (Klas Lestander)
6. 1992 (Albertville)
7. Soviet Union (1968–1988)
8. Norway
9. Erik Kvalfoss
10. Germany
11. 12.5 km pursuit, second part of combined pursuit (placed 56th)
12. Magda Neuner (12.5km pursuit, 15km mass start)

Bobsleigh

1. 2002 (two-woman event only)
2. 1930s (1932)
3. Italy
4. Romania
5. East Germany
6. Soviet Union
7. Switzerland (Gustav Weder, Donat Acklin)
8. Canada and Italy (both timed at 3 mins 37.24 secs)
9. Voneta Flowers
10. Germany
11. Nicola Minichiello and Gillian Cooke
12. Canada

Cross-country (Nordic) Skiing

1. Sweden
2. Finland
3. Sixten Jerberg
4. Italy
5. Bill Koch
6. 15km
7. Bjørn Dæhlie
8. Lyubov Yegorova
9. Combined pursuit
10. Estonia
11. Team sprint
12. Men's 50km

Curling
1. Four payers, two stones each
2. 'House'
3. 1920s (1924)
4. Perth (The Royal Caledonian Curling Club)
5. Canada
6. Switzerland (4–3)
7. Norway
8. USA (8–6)
9. Finland
10. Sweden
11. China (women's bronze)
12. Eve Muirhead

Figure Skating
1. Madge Syers (Edger Syers was her husband)
2. Austria
3. Canada
4. Tenley Albright
5. Triple Lutz
6. Carlo Fassi
7. Backflip
8. Brian Boitano (USA) and Brian Orser (Canada). (Boitano won gold; Orser silver.)
9. Triple axel
10. Michelle Kwan
11. Lithuania
12. Mao Osada

Freestyle Skiing
1. Aeriels, moguls and ski cross
2. 1980s (Calgary 1988)
3. Ballet
4. France (1st Edgar Grospiron, 2nd Olivier Allamand)
5. Uzbekistan
6. USA
7. Norway
8. Five
9. China (Hang Xiaopeng, men's aerials)
10. Switzerland
11. Belarus
12. Australia

Ice Hockey
1. 1920 (at the Summer Games in Antwerp)
2. Canada (1920–1932)
3. Soviet Union
4. USA
5. University of Minnesota
6. Czechoslovakia
7. A shootout (Sweden defeated Canada 3–2 following a 2–2 draw after extra time)
8. USA
9. Italy
10. Sidney Crosby
11. Sweden
12. Finland (Teemu Selänne, 37 points)

Luge

1. Four
2. Kazimierz Kay-Skrzypeski
3. Germany
4. Soviet Union
5. Puerto Rico
6. Brugger (Gunther, Norbert and Wilfried)
7. Georg Hackl
8. Italy
9. Sylke Otto
10. Austria
11. Germany (Felix Loch men's singles, Tatjana Hüfner women's)
12. Latvia

Nordic Combined

1. Ski jumping, cross country skiing
2. 1924
3. Norway
4. Finland
5. Germany
6. Switzerland
7. Ulrich Wehling
8. Germany
9. Japan
10. Sampaa Lajunen
11. Austria
12. 10 km

Short-track Speed Skating
1. 500m
2. Four
3. 14 (They must be at least 15 on July 1 of Olympic year)
4. 1980s (1988)
5. Great Britain
6. Kim Ki-Hoon
7. 1500m (individual)
8. Australia
9. South Korea
10. USA
11. Canada
12. Wang Meng

Skeleton
1. 1920s (1928)
2. Four
3. John Heaton (1928, 1948)
4. Nino Bibbia
5. Great Britain (3rd, 6th, 7th)
6. USA (1st Tristan Gale, 2nd Lee Ann Parsley)
7. Alex Coomber
8. Republic of Ireland
9. Switzerland
10. Shelley Rudman
11. Latvia
12. Germany (Kerstin Szymkowiak 2nd, Anja Huber 3rd)

Ski Jumping
1. USA
2. Rudd
3. Andreas Däscher (Däscher technique)
4. 100 metres
5. Japanese (Yukio Kasaya)
6. Matti Nykänen
7. V
8. Austria
9. Germany
10. Adam Małysz
11. Thomas Morgenstern
12. Simon Ammann (normal hill, large hill)

Snowboarding
1. Ross Rebagliati (Canada)
2. France
3. Switzerland
4. USA
5. Liver
6. Italy
7. Snowboard cross
8. Philipp Schoch
9. Cypress Mountain
10. Shaun White
11. Seth Wescott
12. Netherlands

Speed Skating
1. 10000m
2. Jack Shea
3. 500m (43.1 secs)
4. 1500m (Yevgeny Grishin and Yuri Mikhailov, both USSR)
5. Knut Johanesen (15:46.6)
6. 500m
7. Ard Schenk
8. Thomas Gustafson
9. Bonnie Blair
10. Claudia Pechstein
11. China
12. South Korea (3 golds, 2 silvers)

7. Winter Olympics Numbers

Part 1 – How many?
1. (d) 9
2. (c) 78
3. (d) 18
4. (b) 13
5. (a) 4
6. (c) 150,000
7. (a) 1 (Alexander Cushing, the creator of the resort)
8. (d) 9
9. (d) 14 (following the break-up of the USSR and Yugoslavia)
10. (b) 86
11. (d) 149
12. (c) 39

Part 2 – A Question of Age
1. (c) 54 (54 yr 29 days)
2. (d) 59 (59 yr 155 days)
3. (d) 38 (38 yr 243 days); oldest GB female Winter medallist
4. (b) 11 (11 yr 74 days)
5. (c) 49 (49 yr 155 days)
6. (a) 12 (12 yr 113 days)
7. (b) 33 (33 yr 368 days)
8. (b) 16 (16 yr 261 days)
9. (a) 13 (13 yr 83 days)
10. (c) 15 (15 yr 255 days)
11. (d) 48 (48 yr 307 days)
12. (a) 39 (39 yr 150 days)

Part 3 – Name the Year
1. (b) 1964 (1091 competed in Innsbruck)
2. (c) 1972 (in protest at Communist countries bending the amateurism rules)
3. (d) 2010 (1066 women competed in Vancouver)
4. (b) 1960
5. (c) 1998
6. (c) 1998
7. (a) 1948
8. (d) 1998 (Nagano had 2077 competitors)
9. (c) 1956 (Cortina)
10. (b) 1980 (Robin Cousins, men's singles in figure skating)
11. (c) 1992 (Barcelona and Albertville)
12. (b) 1936 (Germany: Berlin and Garmisch-Partenkirchen)

Part 4 – Placings and scores
1. (d) 46–4
2. (a) 0–0
3. (b) 6th
4. (b) 5th
5. (d) 16–1
6. (c) 4–3
7. (a) 5th
8. (c) 3–1
9. (b) 4–3
10. (a) 5th
11. (a) 5th (6 golds)
12. (b) 3–2

8. Winter Olympics Mixed Bag

Part 1 – First Things First
1. Jeanette Altwegg (Ladies' singles in figure skating, 1952)
2. The RAF
3. 1960 (Squaw Valley)
4. West Germany
5. Ice dancing
6. Senegal
7. Alberto Tomba (giant slalom)
8. Ice hockey
9. Latvia
10. Belarus, Slovakia

Part 2 – Famous Winter Olympians
1. Sonia Henie
2. Jean-Claude Killy
3. Katarina Witt (East Germany), winner of the ladies' singles
4. Michael Edwards
5. Bobsleigh (two-man event)
6. Franz Klammer
7. Sandra Schmirler
8. Divina Galica
9. Bath
10. Robin Dixon (won two-man bobsleigh with Tony Nash, 1964)

Part 3 – Record breakers

1. Norway (107)
2. Bjørn Dæhlie (Norway), 12 (8 gold, 4 silvers)
3. Lidiya Skoblikova (USSR), speed skating, 1960–1964;
   Lyubov Yegorova (Russia), cross-country skiing, 1992–1994
4. Stefania Belmondo (Italy), Raisa Smetanina (USSR)
5. Germany
6. Switzerland
7. Biathlon (4x7.5km relay)
8. Speed skating
9. Bill Johnson (USA), 104.53 km/h (64.95mph) in 1984
10. 14

Part 4 – Trivia Teasers

1. Skeleton
2. First woman to pronounce the Olympic Oath
3. The Walt Disney Corporation
4. Bonnie Blair (Cornwall, New York). She won five golds in
   speed skating, 1988–1994
5. Heating the runners on their sleds
6. Karl Schranz
7. *Cool Runnings* (1993)
8. Zorro
9. Kerstin Szymkowiak (won skeleton silver in 2010)
10. Calgary 1988

Bibliography

1. Printed sources

Baker, Keith – *The 1908 Olympics* (SportsBooks Ltd, 2008)

Buchanan, Ian – *British Olympians* (Guinness Publishing, 1991)

Buchanan, Ian – *Who's Who of UK and GB International Athletes 1896–1939* (NUTS, 2000)

Daniels, Stephanie & Tedder, Anita – '*A Proper Spectacle': Women Olympians 1900–1936* (ZeNaNA Press, 2000)

Duncanson, Neil & Collins, Patrick – *Tales of Gold* (Queen Anne Press, 1992)

Emery, David – *Lillian* (Hodder & Staughton, 1971)

Greenberg, Stan – *Olympic Facts and Feats* (Guinness Publishing, 1996)

Greenberg, Stan – *Olympic Almanack* (SportsBooks Ltd, 2012)

Hampton, Janie – *The Austerity Olympics: When the Games Came to London in 1948* (Aurum, 2008)

McCann, Liam – *The Olympics: Facts, Figures and Fun* (AAPPL Artists' and Photographers' Press Ltd, 2006)

Mallon, Bill & Buchanan, Ian – *Quest for Gold* (Leisure Press, 1984)

Matthews, Peter & Buchanan, Ian – *All-Time Greats of British and Irish Sport* (Guinness Publishing, 1995)

Judd, Ron C – *The Winter Olympics: An Insider's Guide to the Legends, Lore and The Games* (Mountaineers Books, 2009)

Phillips, Bob – *The 1948 Olympics: How London Rescued the Games* (SportsBooks Ltd, 2007)

Phillips, Bob – *Britain and the Olympics, 1896–2010: A celebration of British gold* (Carnegie Publishing Ltd, 2012)

Tibballs, Geoff – *The Olympics' Strangest Moments* (Robson Books, 2004)

Wallechinsky, David & Loucky, Jaime – *The Complete Book of the Olympics* (Aurum, 2008, 2012)

Wallechinsky, David & Loucky, Jaime – *The Complete Book of the Winter Olympics* (Aurum, 2009)

Walters, Guy – *Berlin Games: How Hitler Stole the Olympic Dream* (John Murray, 2006)

Watman, Mel – *Olympic Track and Field History* (Athletics International and Shooting Star Media, 2004)

Watman, Mel – *All-Time Greats of British Athletics* (SportsBooks Ltd, 2006)

2. Online sources

http://www.bbc.co.uk/sport/0/olympics/2012/
http://www.databaseolympics.com/
http://www.guardian.co.uk/sport/olympics-2012
http://www.historyofsports.net/
http://www.independent.co.uk/topic/Olympics
http://www.la84foundation.org/5va/reports_frmst.htm
http://www.london2012.com/
http://www.olympic.org/
http://www.paralympic.org/
http://www.sportal.com/
http://www.sporting-heroes.net
http://www.sports-reference.com/olympics/
http://www.telegraph.co.uk/sport/olympics
http://www.vancouver.com/2010
http://www.wikipedia.org